IZYK MENDEL BORNSTEIN

WITH

AGNIESZKA PISKIEWICZ

MW00907216

B-94

THE SPIRIT OF THE SURVIVOR

A TRUE STORY

This book was published with the support of:

 Yad Vashem
The Holocaust Martyrs' and Heroes' Remembrance Authority
The Foundation for Support of Survivors' Memoirs

 The Azrieli Group

 The Azrieli Foundation

The design, data and editing of this publication are the responsibility of the author.

 Reborn Roots

ISBN: 1-4392-3998-3

EAN: 978-1-4392-3998-8

Copyright © 2009 Yossi Bornstein

All rights reserved. No part of this book may be used or reproduced in any manner whatsoever, electronic, mechanical, photocopying, recording or otherwise, without prior written permission, except for brief quotations embodied in attributed reviews and articles. For more details please contact: yossiborn@gmail.com

Cover design: Shay Rotenberg, Giraphix Studio
Typesetting: Saar Bornstein, Giraphix Studio

"Even though I walk through the valley of the shadow of death, I fear no evil, for You are with me; Your rod and Your staff, they comfort me"
Psalm 23:4

Dedicated to the loving memory of my family murdered during the Holocaust:

my parents

Hanoch Yoseph and Lea Borensztajn (Lenczner)

and my brothers and sisters:

Sara Akresz

Chaim Shlomo

Chana Fagel

Rivka Zysla

Jacob Hersz

Ita Golda

Genuine appreciation to my dear wife, Chedva Bornstein, who supported me in writing this important book, and my dear children:

Lea Goldman

Shoshana Orlansky

Yoseph Bornstein

Zvi Bornstein

and to my grandchildren and great-grandchildren.

"No man is an island entire of itself;
Every man is a piece of the continent, a part of the main;
If a clod be washed away by the sea, Europe is the less,
As well as if a promontory were,
As well as if a manor of thy friend's or of thine own were; Any man's
death diminishes me, because I am involved in mankind,
And therefore never send to know for whom the bell tolls;
It tolls for thee."

John Donne, from Meditation XVII

Foreword

A long time passed since I was asked to write the story of Izyk Mendel Bornstein, until these pages were born. I remembered the shock after reading Nalkowska's *Medallions*, when I was merely few years old. This book changed my perception of the reality forever. Now, after many years, I was supposed to write about this world of which I had learned with disbelief and fear from Nalkowska. This seemed an unfeasible task. I have been fighting with a mixture of emotions resulting in my disability to write. The change came through writing this book. I have been trying to face the words of Elie Wiesel from his Night[1]: "Only those, who experienced Auschwitz know what it was. Others will never know." I have been trying to find the justification to write about the unspeakable pain, which apparently I have no right to know, to those, who, according to Wiesel, will be unable to grasp it anyway. Yet, since July 2007, my life has become the story for the book itself, gently, yet firmly, leading me step-by-step to this moment when I have found myself strong enough to face the challenge. The most important and greatest step was meeting Izyk Mendel Bornstein himself in January 2008 and receiving his appreciation and encouragement during touching moments we shared on the holy *Shabbat* and thereafter.

There are many other important Jewish people I have met in my life, both personally and through book travels, as well as many other Jewish places on my life path: Szczekociny, Zawiercie, Sosnowiec, Czestochowa. All these are now cities of ghosts, of twice murdered souls. Over seventy years ago Nazis invaded the world with their plan to annihilate all Jewry – its people, books, religion, and any symbols carried within. Futile though their attempts proved, the obliteration of the Jewish world still continues. These days the weapons which fire the finishing blows are lack of respect, and first of all, lack of memory. This last itself, the memory, is the most powerful means to save these remains of the world that has gone. The memory of all those who built this world in Poland for almost 1000 years – not the big names of architects, designers or the well-off, but the memory of all those ordinary people making their living in small *shtetls* together with Catholics. All those Polish Jews of whom only some escaped the fire.

---

1   Wiesel, Elie: Night ; Les Eds de Minuit, 1958; English ed. Hill and Wang 2006

Consequently, as an inheritor of this tradition, though born in the world after, I grant myself the right to speak about the unspeakable. I deliberately start with the quotation, already well known by Ernest Hemingway in his *For Whom the Bell Tolls*. These words so accurately describe my own feelings. I feel the loss from the main, a part of the clod, as Donne put it, washed away from Europe during the dark era of Holocaust. This clod has made Europe the less by all her Jewish children and Poland the less by the three million souls of Polish Jews. Their deaths diminish me as a European, as a Pole, as a human. The bell of the Holocaust continues to toll with everlasting sorrow and pain. It tolls for all of us in our hearts, and we can hear it with our empathy.

It is a peculiar experience to be born to the land that so many perceive as a great cemetery. The land deafened to the cry of millions of humiliated, dehumanized, and, finally forgotten souls. The land where Nazi invaders secluded the Jewish population in ghettos for their only "sin"– being Jews. The land where they built camps surrounded with barbed wire, where they brought millions of women, men, children, and babies - healthy, strong and frail alike - all enemies and threats to the new Nazi order of the world. The land where they murdered their "enemies" in gas chambers, first meticulously depriving them of all property, carefully checking for golden teeth and taking off all the hair which suddenly turned out to have a better use as filling for mattresses.

The bells have been tolling for almost seventy years, yet so often we seem to remain deaf to their sounds. In many places it seems the Nazis gained success. Though they lost their war, many times we, Poles, completed their task anyway, ruining the remains of the holy places like Jewish cemeteries and synagogues. These, abandoned after the war, were waiting in vain for their owners to come back. Instead, many times were finally adapted as lands for building and ordinary buildings respectively.

Leon Zelman, a Holocaust survivor from my hometown Szczekociny, writes in his book *After Survival*[1]: "I don't want to write a book about the Holocaust. So much has already been described, analyzed, put into figures about the

---

1   Zelman, Leon with Thurner, Armin: *After Survival*. One Man's Mission in the Cause of Memory (Holmes and Meier Publishers, Inc., 1998)

Holocaust that my recollections add but one more testimony to the best-documented event in the history."

Both Zelman and Bornstein come from the Szczekociny I will never know: a *shtetl* with the number of its Jewish inhabitants dwindling around 50 percent of the total population. We have one thing in common-we were raised there. Yet, I will never have the chance to go to the places they used to go; neither to the synagogue, apparently one of the largest and most beautiful in Poland, nor to any of two cemeteries or *Mykve*. These places no longer exist in Szczekociny and were destroyed only to a certain extent by Nazi invaders during the Second World War. It was we, Polish neighbors, who paved our paths with Jewish gravestones, built plants and houses on the Jewish cemeteries, turned the synagogue to the shed and thus destroyed the traces of our neighbors.

The history turned its circle, and after so many years, I, a young woman living in the *shtetl* which no longer is, transferred to paper the recollections of the one who was not allowed to continue living here. He might have met me in Szczekociny streets in different circumstances, had it not been for the war. Instead, I met Mr. Bornstein in the USA, where he had lived since 1980s. There, so far away from his first home in Szczekociny, he told me his thrilling life story. The book is a fruit of personal writing of Izyk Mendel Bornstein, the interview that I had with him in January, 2008, and numerous private conversations with both Mr. Bornstein and his wife, Chedva.

Izyk Mendel Bornstein and Agnieszka Piskiewicz after the interview, New York, 20th January 2008

Though each survivor has their own amazing story to tell, I believe this one deserves special attention, and not only due to the series of remarkable and unfathomable twists of fate, which bring up the eternal "coincidence versus predestination" issue. This is a story of a man who declares: "I have an obligation to those who came before and will come after me", and who, together with his family, takes the responsibility in his hometown to put the wrong right, honouring the murdered Jewish citizens, and thus, also taking care that the terrible Holocaust events will never occur again. It is the story of a man who taught his children to love the world, though the world seemed not to love him for a time. A sole survivor of a nine-person family, severely war-stricken, Mr. Bornstein used to teach his children: "Remember, if anyone throws a stone at you, throw them back a piece of bread."

In *Dotkniecie Aniola* [1], a rabbi studying *Talmud* during the time of the

---

1   Schonker, Henryk; *Dotkniecie Aniola*, quotation trans. by Agnieszka Piskiewicz, Osrodek Karta, 2005

Holocaust says, "The end will be good … we are not important, it is the Jewish nation that is important and it always comes out of all its crises yet stronger."

Izyk Mendel Bornstein used to share this belief saying, "I believe there is light for Jewish people." With his life he seems to epitomize the persecuted, doomed to non-existence, yet surviving against all odds, and coming out stronger Jewish nation. So meaningfully, the name Bornstein, in Hebrew, means "sapphire", a hard stone so strong that cannot be destroyed, but one that is also used in precious jewelry - a beautiful symbol that can epitomize the entire Jewish nation. Izyk Mendel Bornstein, a sole survivor from his big family, has managed to re- build his still growing family tree. This is also the mystery of the Jewish nation, which was strong enough to preserve its precious, holy books and customs for thousands of years, though so many co-existing cultures died out, forgotten within the years.

Therefore, though so much has already been put into figures, I feel it is still important to put to paper another story of a number: the story of "a man who became a number who became a man[1]". Izyk Mendel Bornstein's name for some time was merely B-94. It was tattooed on his left forearm by Nazis during the darkest period of his life. History has been teaching us numbers – dates, years, battles, victims, injured, maimed, orphaned, and dead. All these statistics are merely cold figures. However, all have stories behind them; all hide experiences, feelings, emotions, fears, expectations but all these were brutally quenched by the meticulously planned action. True history is built not with pure statistics, but with the memory of the survivors, full of suffering and pain.

Numbers, staying a little more at this subject, play an important role within the Jewish culture. Their value is determined by adding all digits together. Thirteen, the number noted in virtually all cultures around the world, has a considerable meaning in Judaism as well. It signifies the age at which a boy matures. There are thirteen principles of Jewish faith, according to Rabbi Moses Maimonides[2]. It is believed God has thirteen Attributes of Mercy;

---

1   Frankl, Victor: Man's Search for Meaning (Washington Square Press, 1985)

2   Rabbi Moses Maimonides, aka Rambam, one of the greatest scholars of *Torah* of all times; a

and finally, it is the numerical value of the word ahava, which is the Hebrew word for "love."

The mysterious number thirteen came also to the life of Izyk Mendel Bornstein. It is the number we receive by adding together nine and four, the digits of his Auschwitz number. The book symbolically has thirteen chapters. There is pain, suffering, injustice, hatred, and death filling the life of Mr. Bornstein. The outcome, however, flourishes with ahava, love. The love that he teaches to his children and spreads in the world; the love that he finds finally in his hometown, where things start to improve. Thirteen, the number of creation, symbolizes the belief of Izyk Mendel Bornstein: "One man can make a difference." One man can bring changes, and create new world. Mysteriously, he finds other people to help him on his way.

For some time, the political situation in Poland stifled many attempts of telling the truth of Holocaust. Many of survivors were unable to speak of what they had gone through. Hence, little was written and published. It seems the time is right now to bring to daylight important testimonies not only to remember, but also to feel. The true cognition may come only through feelings, not through cold logic. And here I return to the beginning of my introduction to challenge Elie Wiesel's belief: if we try to evoke through empathy the understanding of others' fates, we can become wiser from the experience that we had not. Hopefully, in this way it can also help prevent similar incidents in the future.

I would like to take an opportunity to thank here all the family of Bornsteins for letting me be an active participant of this mission and for the amazing, indescribable journey back in time that I witnessed while working on Mr. Bornstein's story. My hometown, Szczekociny, has become a new place for me, once I learned its past from his writing. It has become a magical, peaceful place peopled by two cultures of people, Jews and Christians living their own lives together, yard-in-yard. There must have been better and worse days in this coexistence, I am far from idealization, but it brings pain knowing that world has gone forever and will never come back.

Sadly enough, Mr. Bornstein did not live to see the book published. He

---

Middle Ages philosopher in Morocco, Spain and Egypt

passed away surrounded by his loving wife and four children in the morning of 14 Kislev 5769, (December 11, 2008) in Harrisburg, where he had been living over the last twenty years. According to his wish, he was buried in Petah Tikva, Israel. Although, obviously, he will be sorely missed, judging by his personal experiences of numerous survivals, I daresay it must have been the right timing. Until virtually his last moments, he was listening to the chapters written and adding or correcting the story. I wish to believe that he is satisfied with the final outcome of the book, looking at it from the Beyond.

Only recently have I received a reply from the Holocaust Museum in Washington USA, to whom I would like to thank for their invaluable work in researching worldwide database and finding the documents from the time of Izyk Mendel Bornstein imprisonment, which we published in this book. An additional thanks must go to my father, Gustaw, who enabled and helped us to find the picture of Mendel Bornstein as a pupil in Szczekociny. He, however, was not lucky enough to see this either.

I thank Mr. Bornstein for all the touching meetings and conversations that we shared that changed my life, for all the approval and appreciation from his side.

I would like to thank his wife, Chedva, and his children, Lea, Shoshi, and Zvika for all the support and hospitality. Special thanks to his son, Yossi, who found me on his way of bringing the memory back in Szczekociny and believed I was the right person to tell the story of his dear father and support this project in numerous other ways.

Also, thank you Mor Alkobi, for the translation of Mr. Bornstein's story into English. Without your prompt help, it would have been much more difficult.

Sean Foer, thank you for your wonderful expression, "*The Spirit of the Survivor*" which so perfectly epitomizes the nature of blessed Mr. Bornstein, and which became the title of this special book. Thank you Lisa, Sean's mother, for all your invaluable help in interviewing Mr. Bornstein and writing down his answers.

Thank you, my dear parents, Janina and Gustaw Piskiewicz, for all your help and support.

Thank you Konrad Kostka, my husband, for your patience and understanding.

Thank you, Arnold Reisman, for making a smooth and right path in the last steps of the book.

Thank you Mirek Skrzypczyk for bringing me in the right time to the right place.

Agnieszka Piskiewicz

Szczekociny, January 2009

Introduction

For many years I have been encouraged by my children, my wife Chedva, (long may she live), as well as by those who heard about my fate, to write down my experiences. Hard as everybody tried, however, I thought they would not convince me. Why go back again to these nightmares? What's the use of it? And who would like to hear about that? - I thought. I was certain I would not go back there consciously with my mind, just as I would never set my feet back again on the land where I grew up until the outbreak of the Second World War, which destroyed everything forever and irreversibly. The dreams I had to face at nights were enough. The number on my left arm, B-94, would not let me forget either. The memories had been living their own lives inside me anyway.

In her book Krol Kier znow na wylocie[1] Hanna Krall describes a conversation between a survivor and his wife:

"Why are you so silent?" - she asks.

The husband answers he wants to be silent.

"You are thinking about them again."

"No, I am thinking about myself."

"And what are you thinking?"

"I am pondering."

"What are you pondering on?"

The husband remains silent. She knows it anyway. He is wondering if he should have survived the war. Why him? The sole one from the whole family? Why? For what reason?

Each survivor must face the intermingling emotions of gratitude for being saved and, at the same time, regret for the lost family and pangs of guilt for being alive. This discomfort will forever also disturb my feeling of relief.

---

1   Krall, Hanna; Krol Kier znow na wylocie; trans. by Agnieszka Piskiewicz (Swiat Ksiazki, 2006)

However, I have always known my survival was not a coincidence, though for a long time I had had problems with understanding it. I found a deeper meaning in it, when I eventually decided to make my journey back after sixty years of the tragic events I had to go through. It was always clear God saved me, and thus there must have been a deeper reason in that fact. I understood that better with the visit with my family to my hometown. What I met there helped me realize I had a special mission due to my survival. Persuaded by my oldest daughter, Lea, to start writing down my experiences, and encouraged by the rest of my family, as well, I became convinced to tell the public about my past, to speak about the years since I was born, about my childhood in Szczekociny, Poland, until the outbreak of the Second World War which started on August 31 of 1939. I decided to speak about my life in ghettos and concentration camps until I was liberated by the Americans on May 5, 1945, in Austria, from Gunskirchen, the concentration camp near the city of Wels[1].

At that time of our liberation I was twenty years old and weighed sixty-two pounds. The doctors who examined me then stated clearly, "You are not going to survive. We will, of course, not leave you, but we want you to know, that if by any chance you get better, it will be a miracle from God."

So many other miracles I experienced on my way. So many times I could have died; so many times I was standing face to face with death, where it seemed certain I would not avoid my destiny, yet I survived each time, and was granted another, and yet another chance.

I have an aim with writing this book of my survival from the Holocaust: I want my children, grandchildren and generations that will come to know about the suffering I went through during these years of one of the greatest tragedies of the world. I have an obligation to those who came before and to those who will come after so that the world will know, and such tragedy will never happen again.

I want to fulfill my mission and thank God for protecting me through all these years. I also have a wish to describe my home, *shtetl* Szczekociny, with all its Jewish facilities: a synagogue, cemeteries, *Mykve*, market place,

---

1   Wels, a city in Upper Austria

and library. Nothing remains these days. No Jew lives there either. I wish to revive the memory of this place, and with my words, build the monument of remembering thousands of Jewish people who lived there and built this town, my beloved family included.

I have confidence that Jewish people always survive. Whatever we go through, we never lose hope and God always helps us. There is a light for the Jewish nation and I hope it will never be any Holocaust again, nor will we ever forget this tragic period of 1939 – 1945.

ONE

It was many years before I finally agreed to return to Poland in the beginning of August 2004. During that meaningful visit, I was accompanied by my dear wife and my four children. Fed with the stories from my past that I had told them while they were growing up, my children had become more and more determined to visit the country where I was born and brought up, and where our roots were. Going back was a very difficult decision for me, and for a long time, I firmly rejected their suggestions to do so. "Never am I going to do that," I would say. "I don't want to even hear about that."

Poland was not only my motherland. It was, at the same time, the graveyard of my entire family, my hopes, my expectations, my dreams, my plans, my happiness, and my adolescence. It became the place of my greatest suffering and humiliation, which had inflicted me with incurable, eternal wounds. Time had dressed them with a decent layer, but they will forever keep bleeding under the surface. I would shake inside at any suggestion of entering again into the world of unimaginable tragedy that I came to share with other Polish Jews. I did not feel strong enough to hunt the ghosts of the past in the place that had become a great cemetery of Jewish culture and tradition. My heart was contorted with pain each time I thought about my family, whom I would never see again after the war separated us in 1942.

"How could I go back to the place where all my family was slaughtered? How could I face the places of my eternal horror?" I used to answer my children whenever they asked about going to Poland.

For many years I kept my past to myself. I did not speak about it; I did not feel the need or have the strength to utter what was unspeakable for me. However, what I consciously and persistently was able to successfully push back during the days, I could not control over the nights. Then, my past would come back with double power. Countless times I screamed and woke my wife, who then brought me back to reality. In the nightmares I had to face so often, I was again reduced to the number B-94. I was among the barracks; I was in hiding; I was escaping from carnivorous dogs whose sharp teeth were just a millimeter from my body, and whose ferocious barking accompanied each of my desperate steps. I was escaping from

Nazis, who were running after me, ready to shoot guns, their yelling piercing my vulnerable body. I was escaping persistently, almost every night, and yet, escape I could not.

Mentally and spiritually, just like other survivors, I will forever remain a prisoner of Nazi camps. Never were we given adequate treatment to recover from this horror; I doubt if such treatment exists. The six years of Nazi terror involved not only malnutrition, overwork, and exposure to difficult weather conditions. The Nazis, with their limitless hatred and cruelty, inflicted invisible injuries that scarred our insides; their aim was to deprive us of any hope or positive thoughts. Annihilation was their main goal; dehumanization was the indispensable step toward this process. The difficult comeback after the six years of living in such imprisonment of body, spirit, and mind involves setting ourselves free from the variety of poisonous feelings we had been systematically fed: humiliation, intimidation, fear, and guilt.

Day by day, we lived being constantly reminded in numerous ways that we were not humans and that we did not deserve anything. They, the Nazis, were actually bestowing a great favor on all humankind by getting rid of us Jews, a disgrace of the world. We were shaved, undressed and clothed in striped rags. We all looked the same and not one of us resembled a human being. We were never spoken to; they communicated to us only through constant yelling and shouting. Cold orders were fired at us as quickly as bullets from their machine guns which they used eagerly for any disobedience. We were completely vulnerable to their physical attacks, as well as their severe screams, which murdered our calmness inside. With time, we got used to it and forgot the sound of true human voices. We were not allowed to talk to each other, but even if we had been, we lacked the courage and strength. Therefore, our own voices were also far from normal; they were nothing but apprehensive whispers from our intimidated throats.

The time came that I started to take into consideration the requests of my children, and my strong decision against returning began to wane. I was becoming convinced to let them see the places they had heard of and to let their own children know about my fate. The willingness to share my experiences with a wider group of people was slowly growing inside me, stimulated by the encouragement from the closest members of my family.

One

My wife and my four children were empathic to my fear and reluctance to visit back Poland, but at the same time, they felt a strong need to see Poland and Szczekociny. My children wanted to see the place where I was born and raised by their grandparents with all their aunts and uncles whose names they carry, but whom they could never see, not even in photographs. They wanted to see this land which I was so connected to, which, at the same time, had become forever the graveyard of my happiness.

I myself could not explain how I survived. It remains an unfathomable mystery. In telling stories of my life, the only understanding I have had is that it was a series of miracles from God, week by week, day by day, hour by hour, minute by minute. I believe angels were watching over me all the time. I truly have a lot to thank God for. Thinking about it, I was becoming more and more convinced to let the whole world listen to my story, to learn the truth about how such a nation of culture like Germany could create such a fate for us, and what those, human beings were able to do to other human beings.

Why me? I was the only one from the nine people family to survive. I did not survive because of a secret and hidden place, any shelter that I found that safely secluded me from the rest of the evil world. I survived six Nazi camps. After years I came across a statement shared by some historians saying that those who could survive a few weeks in Plaszow itself were truly lucky. I spent over a year there, surviving not only a typhoid fever epidemic, but also a death sentence by shooting. I survived the Auschwitz concentration camp and subsequent death marches. I faced virtually all of the most difficult moments in the cruelest places built by the Nazis, from which only a few managed to escape. It seems that Fate deliberately took me to the traps with certain death sentences, only to intervene in the last moment, as if to make me realize I was being saved from the inevitable. Had it been only once, I could attribute it to a coincidence, a blessed turn of events. Yet, all these unfathomable circumstances have evoked in me humility toward the Higher Power, toward Life itself. I understood there must be some deeper meaning, some deeper plan, though it was so difficult to accept and so incomprehensible at certain moments of living.

Maybe I survived to establish a family? To keep the roots growing? I wanted

One

to make sense of all that happened to me. I had to leave the country of my ancestors, but still the blood was passed and circulating. I was the only survivor from my entire family, but like most of the other survivors, we kept the Jewish nation alive. Many gave up after the war, they did not want to bring children to the world, which, as they felt, betrayed them. Some did not want to continue living themselves. Yet still, a lot of us and our children, felt an even stronger obligation to grow our family trees and cultivate our culture. So many died, but still the Jewish nation is here. Maybe this was God's plan. I wondered. I would have never imagined the day would come when I would be surrounded with such a big family of four generations, all going their Jewish way, according to the will of God. My four children have given me over twenty grandchildren, and they have already started creating their own families. Certainly, the Nazis had other plans for me.

For a very long time after I was saved I had a problem with coming to terms with the new life circumstances for which I was not prepared. Many gave up, during and after the war. Many accused God. They needed any explanation to what they had witnessed. What I had experienced obviously influenced my religious life for some time as well. We all have been persistently disturbed with the dumb, unanswerable question: why? Many used to say: if God allowed the killing of six million people like that, I do not want to believe in such a God anymore. Naturally, I also had a difficult time accepting the truth about what happened. The more I saw, the more difficult it became. After the liberation, I had to accept not only the facts revealed to everybody, but I also had to come to terms with the fact that the hopes I had cherished shyly inside were not to be fulfilled. My prayers were not answered: I was left alone, the only survivor from all my family, with nothing except the striped, worn out, filthy clothing I was left wearing at the end. I had no home to go back to, no brother or sister, no parents.

Of course I rebelled, cast unanswerable questions, and cried. I felt lonely and abandoned physically, as well as deep inside. It seemed nothing could heal my anguish after what I had witnessed and experienced myself; nothing could soothe my longing after my beloved family and the peaceful living that had been torn out from us. The knowledge that there was no coming back to what I had left in Szczekociny was at times even more difficult to accept than the facts of what had happened to me and the

One

Jewish world. I myself was trying to find a sense, a deeper meaning of what I saw and heard; six million Jewish people annihilated from the surface of the earth: six million people treated worse than animals - robbed, gathered in a closed area, experimented on, starved, humiliated, dehumanized, and finally burnt in crematoria when they had nothing more to offer for their tormentors. Can anyone find a meaning in that? Can anyone understand? What meaning can there be in casting babies from windows or into a fire, as Nazis used to do while watching their mothers' reactions? How does one live after breathing the smell of burnt bodies of innocent people - men, women and children? Why? What wrong had we done to deserve such hatred and indifference of the world? What happened to my own family? Did they suffer much before they were murdered? Where and how exactly did their lives come to a sad end? I know I will never be given an answer for these questions that plague me deeply.

However, positive events in my later life, time passing by, as well as the *Torah*, helped me to recover slightly, enough to pray again. I forgot many things during the war, but I kept most of the prayers in my heart. During those difficult six years, I kept praying whenever I could. Obviously, I could not wear my *tefilim*[1] and *tallit*[2] I could not stop and pray visibly for others either, but I said holy words inside my heart. It soothed the pain a little, and it gave me some hope.

I remembered from the Bible that there were always some who wanted to destroy us, the Jewish people. There were always those, who wanted to take our faith and beliefs from us; they wanted to take our lives. Even so, we have always continued. We, the Jewish people, were attacked again; again our enemies, the Nazis, tried to take our faith and beliefs, remorselessly taking so many of our innocent lives. Yet, the Jewish nation survived again, hoping to be able to preserve their traditions and go the Jewish way again. Even though many rebelled about their origin, which happened to bring them nothing but suffering, the Jewish nation was still there; maimed,

1   *Tefilim*, Hebrew, two small leather boxes containing scrolls from *Torah* which are strapped to the left arm, pointing to the heart, and forehead, pointing to the mind and thoughts, by Jewish men for daily prayer

2   *Tallit*, Hebrew, a prayer shawl worn while reciting morning prayers and in the synagogue on *Shabbat* and holidays; attached to it, there are knotted fringes known as *Tzitzit*

decimated, but strong enough to continue.

"This trip will be for all the generations," I decided one day, finally making my mind to go back to Poland. I did not know at that time how much I was right and how strongly this decision would influence my family.

My friends, having heard of this choice, came with strong advice against it. "It will not make you any good," they kept saying. "You are losing a lot of money just to suffer again and feel a great pain. You should not go."

I weighed all possible pros and cons in my mind. It was one of the most complicated decisions in my life. Apparently, just a journey, it involved much more than simple travelling to a different place. It would be at the same time a profound journey inwards, to my deepest, strongest, and most intimate thoughts and feelings, born during the events that shaped me into man I am today. To the same extent, it would be a journey backwards to my childhood, my adolescence, my family life, and to what came after, which destroyed my worldview, and my sense of safety forever.

Preparing for the trip, I kept thinking of my life, trying to embrace its numerous, unexpected turns of fate. I left Poland still during the time of occupation. After the liberation and treatment I had to undergo due to the emaciation of my body, I decided to head for the only place suitable in my mind for Jews at that time, Palestine. I was trying hard to organize my new life there. It was difficult, as I was completely alone and with nothing apart from what I was wearing. I managed, however. I started my own family, which became my most precious treasure for all my life. I became an active soldier, a fighter, and a medic for IDF[1] for twenty-two years. Starting in a *Kibbutz* [2] with no personal belongings when I arrived in 1946, over the years I managed to build a calm, safe life for my family, giving us all the feeling of security.

It was not easy in the beginning when I decided to move to the United

---

1   Israel Defense Forces; military ground and air forces, and navy for Israel

2   *Kibbutz*, Hebrew "gathering", a communal living of community in Israel based originally on agriculture, today comprising other forms of industry, based on socialism and Zionism ideas; less than 5 percent of Israelis live these days in this way

States in 1982 either, but again, with God's help, I succeeded. Since then, I had lived a calm life in the American city of Harrisburg, Pennsylvania. I found there a good Jewish environment and community; I felt appreciated in the synagogue and respected for my past tragic experiences. Many people saw God's Providence in my fate and me as a chosen one. Some would come and ask me to bless them, which I found truly touching.

My apprehensiveness to go back to Poland was justified with what I had experienced when Adolf Eichman's [1] process was started in the beginning of the nineteen sixties. I followed its every step, and kept listening carefully to each update of the news on the radio. Eichman, a Nazi and SS officer, was one of the main organizers of the so-called *Endlosung* [2], the plan of exterminating all the Jewish nation, and the one who postulated and recommended using Zyklon B, a cyanide–based insecticide used by the Nazis in gas chambers in extermination camps. It facilitated their murdering process, killing over one million victims who thought they were going to showers. His name itself used to bring a lot of emotions to the world of survivors. We, who came from different extermination camps, saw it as a hand of justice coming to revenge our suffering, and all those innocent victims of not only Zyklon B, but all Nazi rule. However, the process was a big unknown; the defense was trying different arguments to question its legitimacy. This time truly influenced my nervous system, and drained my strength away. I kept asking myself questions: "Will he face the justice or escape it, just like most of Nazis? Will it change anything?"

One night during that difficult time, when still it was not certain what would happen to Eichman, I couldn't sleep because of nerves accompanying this situation. I got up and went to my children's room. Always I used to check if everything was all right with them, to make sure they didn't need anything and that they were covered with blankets. That night, however, when Eichman's process was running, I did not come back to my bedroom.

---

1   Adolf Otto Eichman, (1906 – 1962) charged with managing mass deportations of Jews to extermination camps. After the war, he was found by agents of Mossad in Argentina and brought secretly to Israel, where he was sentenced to death and hanged, his body burnt and spread over the Mediterranean Sea outside the territory of Israel

2   *Endlosung*, German; The Final Solution of the Jewish Question, a terminology used by Adolf Hitler referring to the mass killing of the Jewish nation

I had not even managed to cover all my children properly, when I passed out between their beds. I know what happened later from my wife, who woke up because of the significant dream she had. "I saw your mother," she told me, which by itself was curious, as obviously she had never had a chance to meet her. "Without realizing much, I told her, '"He is coming to you,"' and she replied, '"No, he is not."' It happened three times, and after her third answer, I woke up and realized you are not in bed, so I got up and found you in the children's room, lying between their beds unconscious." Thanks to this intervention, I was taken to the hospital, where I spent a few days with a diagnosis of nervous attack. I had been unconscious already for a few hours when my wife found me. Scared enough by my condition, she ran out to the nearest neighbors to call an ambulance.

Could it be it was indeed my dear mother, who came to rescue me? It sounds completely incredible, but wasn't my all life incredible by itself? Wasn't my survival incredible, with all its surprising events on the way and their results? Can we judge what is real and what is not, what is probable and what not? Is it probable to live in a world, where one nation rises against another culture and builds closed camps, where its people experiment on those persecuted ones, with the aim of creating a perfect, biological man? Where they rush with inventing the quickest and most effective way of exterminating their bodies? Where they use their hair for producing material and their fat for soap? Isn't this scenario incredible by itself?

I survived the six years of Nazi occupation thanks to nothing else but inexplicable interventions, I believe, from the Above. It took me a long time of profound endeavors to be able to function somehow in everyday life and to smother my pain. Why go back and risk losing what I rebuilt inside me with my strong efforts? Why should I face again the places that became my worst nightmares? Though I wasn't completely convinced, I did not want to change my mind again. I promised my children; they needed to see it, and that was most important. I was persuading myself. There was some voice inside me, against all the logic, which kept encouraging me to do this apparently irrational thing and take this journey back.

Already at the airport, I suddenly felt scared. I thought of the Poland I had left sixty years ago. I heard the voices of my friends, advising me against returning, and felt a strong urge to give up this idea, which suddenly seemed to me completely irrational. I was still not balanced. I was torn between the curiosity and willingness to face the challenge, and enter this old world, with the fear inside, which still had a lot to say as for my decisions.

"I don't know if this is a good idea," I said sharing my doubts with the family, ready to go back home.

I stayed where I was only thanks to their true understanding, help, and support. I could rely on them, as always. I tried, with their help, to calm down. They must have realized the power of the fear I had deep inside, which began to take control over me. Sixty-five years had already passed since the war started, and I was going back for the first time. I did not know what to expect there. Thoughts kept running through my head. How will I react? What will happen? What will I see there after all this time? The plane took off, bringing me to where everything started and at the same time where everything finished in a way. My mind was, in the meantime, starting the journey backwards, taking me into the depth of my memories.

Bornstein family during their first visit to Szczekociny in 2004. From the left: Chedva Bornstein, Lea Goldman, Izyk Mendel Bornstein, Shoshana Orlansky, Zvi Bornstein and Yossi Bornstein

TWO

I was born on March 17, 1924, the fifth of seven children, to my parents, Chanoch Yoseph and Lea Borensztajn. I was named after my late grandfather, Izyk Mendel. We used to live in a small *shtetl* [1], Szczekociny, which we used to call, in Yiddish, Chekocin. It was a peaceful and lovely town in the southern part of Poland, approximately eighty kilometers from Krakow, Kielce and Katowice, respectively, the biggest cities in the area. It was not a big place. There were 5500 people approximately, and at least half of them were Jewish. In such a small place, we used to know one another quite well and lived, in fact, like one big family. We didn't feel anti-Semitism at all. We lived together, Christians and Jews, as good neighbors, respecting one another and depending on one another to a certain extent to make our livings. Most of the families in my street which, at that time, was called Sienkiewicza and these days has been named Koscielna were Jewish. However, our next door neighbors were the Christian family of Wojtasinski, the owners of a bookshop, who prided themselves on their big collection of books. Even though they were not Jewish, we used to live as one family and we were very happy and proud to have such intelligent and nice neighbors. I befriended their daughter, Kazimiera. She was the same age as me; we were schoolmates. As children, we used to play together in our gardens where we had an enjoyable time. In their backyard, they had fruit trees. I remember long branches of their apple tree and apples falling into our garden from the heavy branches of the tree growing on their side of the fence. They would always say, "What is ours is yours." We ate the juicy fruits with pleasure. In the warm summer evenings, our mothers used to meet after long, tiring days and sit on the steps of their bookshop to rest a while. Many times other women would join them to exchange some opinions and harmless gossip from the town.

A few houses from ours in the other direction lived the Zuckerman family. I remember their little daughter, Jadzia, strolling proudly on the pavement next to our windows. She always wore her beautiful clothes and had a meticulous haircut. She seemed to me a little spoiled princess at that time.

---

1   *Shtetl*, from the Yiddish word *shtot* meaning town; refers to a small town with dominant Jewish community in pre–Holocaust Europe

Two

She was much younger than me; therefore, we did not know each other well. By a quirk of fate, several dozen years after I had been forced to leave Szczekociny during the war, I talked to Yehudit Gold, a Szczekociny survivor, standing next to Jadzia's family house. We tried to help each other recall certain places and people to find what we could have in common. "Do you remember this girl?" I asked her trying to describe what I could remember best about Jadzia. "She could be your age actually, and she lived somewhere here as well." Yehudit looked at me, amused and surprised at the same time. "It was me! Everybody called me Jadzia at that time!" I couldn't believe I learned this in such circumstances and hoped she was not offended by my description of her as a little girl.

Not far from us lived Mr. Rozenblat's widow. People used to come and buy seats for wagons from her. Another neighbor was Mr. Potas, who had a shop with school items. Finally, opposite the street, there was a restaurant belonging to Mr. Brygalski. We did not go there, since it was not kosher. However, we could always hear the music coming from the inside. At times people drank too much alcohol and small fights resulted. The police were therefore, also there often and not as guests. They would come to intervene and restore the order.

My parents owned two neighboring houses, numbers five and seven. The first one was one-storey, wooden and old. The other was red-bricked, divided into the living section of our nine people family, shops, and the letting area. My parents rented some space for the Goldberg family, who had a shop and also lived there. My father originally came from Wodzislaw, a small town forty kilometers from Szczekociny, with quite a significant Jewish community too. He moved to Szczekociny when he married my mother. Since both my parents came from Orthodox religious families, they were introduced to each other by some matchmakers. My parents, in their later lives, also used to do matchmaking. My mother's family, Lenczners, traded with suits. Their children, however, continued the family tradition outside Szczekociny, mainly in Bedzin and Sosnowiec, where they moved and opened their shops.

Sienkiewicza, where we lived, was quite a small street. In a way it led to the two town temples. To the right, passing the nearby and the only market square in the town, which we used to call, in Polish, rynek, there was our beautiful synagogue. On the other end of the street, there was an impressive Catholic church, whose bells I used to hear very well, along with the singing and praying during Catholic holy days. Obviously, I was never inside there[1]. However, we would watch with interest the most important ceremonies taking place there from our balcony overlooking the street. During important Christian holidays, so many people would gather that they had to stand around the church, since there was no more space inside; it was no matter that the church was a big building. I liked watching soldiers who would come to participate in important ceremonies, dressed and armed according to the Polish army traditions. During the week, however, we did not hear much from the church at our home, though we lived very close to it.

Sienkiewicza (Koscielna) Street and the Catholic Church in Szczekociny before the Second World War. On the left, the white buildings, Izyk Mendel Bornstein's home

Our home was very traditional and warm. Each of us, children, had his or her tasks every day after school to help father and mother around the

---

1   According to *Halacha*, i.e. Jewish law, Jews are not allowed to enter Christian churches, since entering this religious experience of the belief into Holy Trinity implies questioning the Jewish belief in One and Only God

house as much as we could. I remember running to bring fresh milk home; it was milked right to my can. What a delicious taste it was! After some time in a glass, thick cream gathered on top. It was such a good quality; we used to make our own butter from it. Every evening, when everybody was already home, we ate together at the big table in the dining room. My father had his place at the head of the table, and nobody else, not our guests nor ourselves, ever sat there. At that time, father was the most respectable person in our home. I remember that he, not the children, always got a double portion of meals, which was the sign of the respect we had for him. We used to prepare our own food, so that everything was fresh. Nowhere in the town's shop or bakery could one get *Challah* [1]. Women used to bake their own at homes; so did my mother. Each *Shabbat* [2] and each festival our house would become filled with tempting smells coming from the kitchen. Generally Jews in the *shtetl* were known for preparing good food. On Thursdays and Fridays, when women were started preparing food for *Shabbat*, we would not hide the smells coming from our houses The streets would fill with the smells coming through the windows of Jewish houses and these usually were chicken soup, fried fish, roast beef, cocoa cakes, cheesecakes, and apple cakes. Festive dishes were always very important for us during *Shabbat*, and Christians used to like our food indeed. Some asked for recipes and prepared similar dishes at their homes.

I will forever remember life in our *shtetl* as a very simple and quiet. Local shops and traders satisfied our material needs. There was a splendid library with numerous books both in Yiddish and Polish; they covered a wide field of interest, and everybody found something for themselves there. We had shops, restaurants, schools, and places to pray. Szczekociny was a truly peaceful and beautiful town. In summer it would welcome guests from bigger cities such as Bedzin, Sosnowiec, and even Lodz and Warsaw. Some would come to visit with their families; some would come to pray in the synagogue; others simply were attracted to our clean air and peace and

---

1   *Challah*, a braided bread eaten during *Shabbat* and some other festivals

2   *Shabbat*, Saturday, the seventh day of rest commemorating God's rest after the creation process, during which no work can be done; starts on Friday evening with blessing the candle light by a woman, and followed by man's blessing the bread (*Challah*), and wine during ceremonious dinner and lasts until Saturday dusk

quiet. There was a tiny lake, where people loved spending their time with all the families sitting on the green grass, catching sunrays onto their skin, and resting after hectic weekday life.

On the outskirts of the town there was a beautiful, big palace, the property of Mr. Jan Ciechanowski. He was a rich and influential person, an ambassador of Poland in the United States of America in the 1920s and later again during Hitler's occupation. He was respected in the town, and his position was unquestionable, but it did not influence his modesty and virtuous character. I remember walking in the street with my father and watching him passing in the carriage hitched to horses. I will never forget seeing him taking his hat off and bowing first to my father, regardless of his position.

People loved the palace, which used to bring them not only rest, but also a lot of joy. Senatorska Street, which came out of the town's centre and led directly to the palace, would grow crowded during weekends with families walking slowly toward the old, impressive building. On Saturday afternoons, Jewish parents strolled with their excited children toward the park and forests surrounding the palace. Sundays looked much the same, but now these were Christians who were visiting on their holy day.

The palace had a beautiful garden in front of it with plenty of beautiful flowers growing around and spreading far their pleasant scents. They mixed with the smells of trees from the park and a dense forest that was stretching behind, inviting us to taste its wild fruits. We loved blueberries especially. The forest itself was overgrown with trees, and it was easily to lose the way. We used to take a compass with us not to get lost, but we were not allowed to use it during *Shabbat*; therefore, everybody was careful then not to go in too deep. At the same time, most would not resist the taste of fresh fruits. For those who preferred not to go inside the forest surrounding the palace, there were numerous apple trees with juicy fruits that we were allowed to pick as well.

Children had the most fun with the animals that were kept by the owners of the palace. They used to breed cattle and horses there too, and all the youngest rushed to look at the young calves, trying to touch them, if possible. The greatest joy was to find a feather of one of the numerous turkeys and ducks strolling there. The bigger and more colorful feathers they found, the happier children were when coming back home. People would bring blankets to sit on, sometimes a little food to eat while spending their time in nature. Everybody found something there for themselves: resting on the grass and talking with family and friends, tasting fruits, strolling around, playing with small animals, breathing fresh air - the place offered a true rest for the body and soul. No wonder it attracted so many families, especially during warm, summer days.

The market square was surrounded with various shops and restaurants, also mostly Jewish. They provided us with everything we needed for our everyday life. There was no need to travel anywhere; our shops sufficed completely. All local traders looked forward to Wednesday, which used to be the most important market day. Then they were able to earn their living indeed. Each week, on Wednesday, unless it coincided with an important Catholic or Jewish religious festival, rynek would become vibrant with loud voices, and various smells, and crowded with buyers and sellers. Farmers from all nearby villages used to come with their cattle, horses, and chickens; many brought dairy, eggs, and meat produced at their farms. They either sold these, or tried to exchange them for other products necessary for their existence. Catholics and Jews traded and exchanged goods together. Many of us used to go and look around the place and enjoy this pleasantly hectic atmosphere.

Szczekociny's Market Place (Rynek) before the Second World War. On the left, the monument of Tadeusz Kosciuszko

In the centre, a monument protruded proudly. It was the figure of General Tadeusz Kosciuszko[1], built in 1917 with community funds. It was our common Jewish and Christian pride, for Kosciuszko used to treat both cultures with due respect. During Christmas time, when Christians used to decorate the town with Christmas trees and various ornaments, they would also put colorful lamps on the monument, making Kosciuszko a more colorful and cheerful figure. During our Jewish festival of *Purim* [2], the place was filled with Jewish families, adults and children, all happy and cheerful, telling jokes. All of us would wear different masks and costumes; it was at times difficult to recognize who was who behind the disguise. Some would walk on crutches of four to five meters high, and usually, there was a big, brown bear figure dancing around as people around clasped their hands and laughed.

Purim in Szczekociny was a truly happy event involving the whole Jewish community, gathering us all together in our market square for common joy and celebration. On the eve of the festival, our family house would draw together all the close neighbors, who would come to listen to my dear father, Rabbi Hanoch Yoseph Borensztajn, read ceremoniously from the *Book of Esther* to a special melody. We, the children, would listen to it with pleasure, and wait with our graggers to make noise whenever we heard the word *Haman*. After that, we would all enjoy a wonderful *Purim* feast of *Gefilte fish* [3] and *Kreplach*.[4] All the house would fill with the merry voices singing *Purim* songs. I will never forget the view of my beloved father during one such celebration, when suddenly he stood up on his chair at the head of the table and started dancing. His dance lasted around ten minutes and

---

1   Tadeusz Kosciuszko, (1746 – 1817) Polish and American general, leader of the national insurrection of 1794, participant of American War of Independence of 1776

2   *Purim*, Jewish festival celebrated on the 14th day of the month *Adar*, which corresponds to the period of February – March, during which the *Book of Esther* is read, gifts are given to the poor, and feasts with wine drinking take place. It is the joyful event of commemorating saving of Jewish nation from the plot of *Haman*, a Persian royal vizier, by the Queen of Persian Empire, *Esther*. During the reading of *Esther's Book* (*Megilla*), whenever *Haman*'s name is mentioned, children make noise with various noisemakers, the so-called *Purim* graggers

3   *Gefilte fish*, filled fish; poached fish patties made from mostly carp or pike mixed with various spices, eggs, onions and bread

4   *Kreplach*, small dumplings filled with ground meat or mashed potatoes, usually served in chicken soup

we all were not able to refrain our laughing, seeing our father in such a situation. Even my mother seemed shocked to see for the first time such talent from her husband. Probably my father had drunk too much wine or schnapps at the time, but he surprised us all and brought about a lot of fun.

The festival itself would bring us the same amount of joy as the preparations for it. A few days before, children started their preparations in our school. We used to bring cartons, paper, color pencils, and pieces of different materials. With the help of our teacher, we used to prepare our own masks, cutting proper shapes from cartons and then putting colors onto them. We would cut small holes for our eyes and lips - to be able to see through and breathe. It was not that easy at all, but it used to bring us a lot of excitement and fun. Finally, the masks were ready and we tried them on, happy we could not recognize one another. Having finished that task, we would prepare our rattles out of string and some pieces of wood. They were truly effective and used to make a lot of noise; if there was any child trying to sleep during the joyful evening of *Purim*, they had to wait; our rattles were too noisy, especially when accompanied by our feet stomping. We couldn't wait to wear our hand-made masks and go to other houses with our merry hearts singing traditional *Purim* songs in Yiddish.

Apart from *Purim*, we children loved the eight-day celebrations of Festival of Lights, *Chanukah*. It starts on the 25th day of the month Kislev, according to our Jewish calendar, which corresponds to the period of December, and hence it coincides with Christian Christmas. So it happened that while we Jews, lit our eight candles, one more each day[1], our Christian neighbors prepared their Christmas trees, and their ornaments and candles, and we all celebrated as our traditions told us. I remember one Christmas time a teacher came to me together with a priest. I knew him a little from the school, as he used to come to teach Christian children religion during the time we, Jewish children, were studying with our Rabbi. The relations between these two were also all right. I had a very good voice and I liked singing, which was always rewarded with good marks at school. Probably the priest asked the teacher to take him to boy with a good singing voice. I

---

1 *Chanukah* commemorates the happy events in the 2nd century BC at the time of *Maccabean Revolt* when the wicks of the *Menorah* miraculously burned for eight days in the Temple, though there was only enough sacred oil for one day

was asked to come and sing in a choir during Christian church ceremonies. I felt both surprised and appreciated. It was on the one hand an honor for me that they valued my singing so much that they came to a Jewish boy. On the other hand, they must have realized I came from a religious family and, according to my rules, I was not allowed to enter and pray in church. I had to refuse, which they clearly did not like, but I was faithful to my religious obligations.

Both Christmas and *Chanukah* made the *shtetl* children's hearts merry with their celebrations. Christian children had their presents and carols, and we Jewish children, could hardly wait all year to play the card game of 21 and have fun with the spinning top. My elder sister, Rivka, would sit with us and make sure we didn't fight with one another while we were playing. We all would get equal amounts of money, and while playing, we would try to win and get other's cash, which at times resulted in some quarrels; everybody wanted to win. Rivka took care the game was fair, and if there was any argument, she would make the final decision. We could sit and play for long hours and truly enjoy our time. We stopped only when our eldest sister, Sara, entered with plates filled with *Chanukah* delicacies. We all rushed to taste sweet pancakes and latkes she would fry with my mother in the kitchen.

Sara used to be like a second mother for us, and we respected her position. She spent most of her time together with my mother; she helped her to cook, do the shopping and laundry. I remember people outside often took them for sisters whenever they would walk in the street. My mother used to be a very elegant, slim woman. She took care of herself indeed, and she looked young. We loved her and respected very much. We never dared to go directly to her if we needed something. First, we would go to Sara. We needed her permission to go and disturb mother and talk to her. If she decided not to let us do something, there was no complaining; we had to accept it. We recognized each decision, though we did not always like it, obviously. With all other siblings, we were taught to respect each other, especially according to age.

During *Chanukah*, my mother would buy a few huge geese to prepare goose fat. Each of us had some duties connected to this process. The preparations started with visiting the slaughterer, who would kill the geese according to the Jewish law of *Kashrut* [1]. While cutting the geese, we checked carefully if everything was right inside, and if the bird was healthy. In case of doubt, we would ask the rabbi. If some of the *Kashrut* rules were broken, we would buy other geese, and sell these cheaply to a restaurant three doors down the street from our house. It was not a Jewish restaurant, so they did not have to follow such complicated rules as we did. Usually, though, everything was all right, and we happily proceeded with our preparations. All the feathers were made into large quilts prepared by women and left as presents for daughters getting married; my mother would sit thus with my sisters next to the fire during long winter evenings and sew their dowry while talking and joking. In the process of preparing goose fat for *Chanukah*, my duties were immersion and salting. Obviously at that time we had no running water at home; no one did. So, we would bring it from a nearby pump. It was filtered to make it kosher. I always used to go with two buckets.

We would later hang the two geese in one of the two kitchen windows; their panes were frozen, so they served as temporary fridges. When finally the fat was separated and it came time for the cooking, the whole house was slowly filled with such pleasant smells that teased our noses; we all couldn't wait to taste goose fat on fresh bread. Then, we would all sit together, the children and parents, watching *Chanukah* candles light the window facing the street. We would sing festival songs and eat fresh bread with the long awaited goose fat. We would look at each other happily, equally enjoying the festival and our presence.

Autumn used to fill the town with a completely different atmosphere with its High Holidays of *Rosh Ha'shana*, the Jewish New Year [2], and *Yom*

---

1   *Kashrut*, a set of Jewish dietary laws defining which food is kosher, meaning fit or non-kosher, i.e. treif. Many of the basic laws are derived from the *Torah*. The most important rules concern the permission of eating only certain species, i.e. mammals that both chew and have cloven hooves, have to be slaughtered by a trained person in a single, continuous movement with a sharp knife avoiding animal's pain. All the blood needs to be removed. Fish is accepted only if it has scales and fins. Meat and milk cannot be mixed during one meal or cooked in the same utensils

2   *Rosh Ha'shana*, Jewish New Year, symbolic anniversary of the creation of the world. According to the Jewish Calendar on the 1st day of *Tishrei* which corresponds to mid September. According to the belief, God inscribes each person's fate for the coming year into the book of life or death;

Kippur, the Day of Atonement[1]. A week before *Rosh Ha'shana*, we would start our apologies. We would ask for forgiveness to repent for the sins we committed in the previous year, so that when our fate would be judged ten days later, on *Yom Kippur*, God would seal us in the Book of Life. Jews in Szczekociny would go to three different places mainly to say *Selichot*, our penitential prayers[2]. We would gather in the synagogue, and in our places for religious studies: *Beit Midrash* [3], and Chasidic *Stibel* [4]. Each Jewish community had a helper in a synagogue that was responsible for calling for prayers, pronouncing the beginning and end of festivals, and other religious duties. He was called shames, in Yiddish, from the Hebrew word shammash. During the preparations for the High Holidays, at the break of the dawn, when there was still dark outside, a shames would come and knock with a hammer at the wooden gates of the Jewish houses, calling out in Yiddish, "Rise and say *Selichot*!" We all obediently followed this call and emerged into the atmosphere, asking for forgiveness for our deeds.

On the eve of the festival, my father took my brother Jacob and me to the *Mykve*, a ritual bath[5], where we purified our bodies and souls. When the turn would come for women, my mother would go with the girls. We all started to feel the importance of the festival in the air. After the *Rosh Ha'shana*

---

prayers in the synagogue take place, *shofar*, the ram's horn, is blown; festive meals are eaten; no work is done; and people dress white clothes. It is the first of the High Holidays, the Ten Days of Repentance during which people try to amend their behavior and repent for sins done to God and one another, asking for forgiveness. This period concludes on *Yom Kippur*. According to the tradition, prayers are cited near water, where pockets are symbolically emptied symbolizing casting one's sins

1   The Day of Atonement; the most solemn and important of Jewish holy days, finishing the period of Ten Days of Repentance, observed on the tenth day of *Tishrei*, i.e., mid September. Traditionally, it is the day of rest and fasting, abstaining from physical pleasures and intensive praying; according to the belief, God seals people's fate on this day. At the end of it, after repentance and confessions of guilt, people are absolved by God

2   *Selichot* is from Hebrew selicha, forgiveness; Jewish penitential prayers that are said especially within the period of High Holidays, i.e. *Rosh Ha'shana* and *Yom Kippur*

3   *Beit Midrash*, Hebrew, a study hall, usually distinct from a synagogue but can refer to the synagogue too. It has most important books for religious studies

4   *Stibel*, Yiddish, literally a room; refers to a place of religious studying

5   *Mykve*, Hebrew, a ritual bath serving for purification of people and objects; must have enough running water to cover the body and the water must come in prevailing proportion from natural sources, like rain, spring, river or lake

sermon, we heard a *shofar* sound, reminding us about our obligations to God and of the coming Day of Judgment. It would fill us all with awe and respect of the unknown. The eyes of all were filled with tears and respect. People used to remind me of angels at that time, all of them wearing white clothes, white hats and belts. It created a mysterious atmosphere.

Later, we had a festive dinner at home. We would eat first of all apples with honey, to make the new coming year sweet, *Gefilte fish*, potato dishes, and different types of cakes. We would all sit at the table and listen to the father's explanation of what our observances mean. We would all feel fearfulness listening to his words: "Tonight, all of us will pass in front of God Almighty like a flock of sheep; God will judge who will live and who will die." We all wanted to believe we would have *Chatima Tova*, and that we would be sealed in the Book of Life![1] The Day of Atonement, *Yom Kippur*, which finish the period of Ten Days of Repentance, is the most solemn and important festival for each Jew. It always used to be a very important for me as well. Since my childhood, it inflicted in me peculiar feelings and emotions, filled me with awe and humility. However deep it was, though, as a child, sitting at the table with my family and listening to my father with respect, even in my wildest dreams I did not suspect what Fate would bring us with *Yom Kippur* of the following years. The ones to come would profoundly change my entire life, my worldview, and my perspective on existence.

My dear father, just like his family, was *Chassid*, unlike, however, most Jews in Szczekociny. It meant that he belonged to a religious movement within the Orthodox Judaism, which followed Rabbi Israel ben Eliezer, known as Ba'al Shem Tov, who wanted to revive Judaism with joy and true spirituality, seeing the religion as too much academic. There were many different groups of *Chassid*ism in Poland before the war, each followed their own dynasty and its rules. My father's family belonged to the Sochaczewer Chasidic Movement. He used to go and pray in Radomsko, a bigger town than Szczekociny, located close to Czestochowa, whereas his father would pray at Alexander Stibel. When I was around nine years old, a new, splendid *Beit Midrash* was built. It used to function as a place

1 *Chatima Tova*, Hebrew, literally: good final sealing; being inscribed in the Book of life

for praying and studying, but most of all, people used to sing psalms there. Most of those who would come there were not *Chassidic*, they had their own halls. As a *Chassid*, I never went into the building of *Talmud Torah* for Zionist children and I didn't meet their teachers either. They had their own traditions and programs, which were also very good, I am certain.

My father truly took care of my education. As he was busy with work, like many other men, he could not spend as much time as he would wish studying. Therefore, he used to talk to me and listen to what I studied and learned. He would enquire about the religious rules concerning treating employees well and sharing with the poor in order to live according to God's commandments. I was so proud and happy to share my knowledge with him. I am grateful to him and all the teachers I had who took care of my religious education. It was thanks to them that I was able to pray during difficult moments of my life, which brought me some comfort. I went to *Cheder* [1] for the first time when I was four years old. There were quite a few such schools in our small town; a lot of parents decided to educate their sons in a religious way. I remember being a small boy and starting each day in the morning by thanking God for giving me my soul back, saying *Mode Ani* [2], but I could easily say longer prayers too, even *Kiddush Levanah* [3] which is said as a sanctification of the moon. I remember reciting psalms with my dear father. We both knew many of them by heart, and it gave me so much joy to sing and pray with him.

Actually, I knew most of the important prayers by heart. I never forgot those who shaped my religious life while I was growing up. We had three study rooms in our *Cheder*, according to the age of the children. We started at the age of four or five with Mr. Litvak. He spent three years with me in

---

1   *Cheder*, Hebrew, "a room," the traditional religious elementary teaching the basics of Judaism and Hebrew to boys, in the house of the teacher, a *Melamed*. Girls were educated at homes by their mothers

2   *Mode Ani*, a Jewish prayer said in the morning right after waking up to thank God for returning souls. According to the belief, during the night, when the body is sleeping, the soul is coming to God, hence saying thanks to God for returning it back in the morning and giving another day to live and do good

3   *Kiddush Levanah* is a sanctification of the moon; the ceremony usually takes place after *Rosh Chodesh*, i.e. the beginning of the new month and new moon. The ritual usually takes place at the conclusion of Sabbath, at night with the shining moon with the series of prayers recited

Cheder. Then, being around eight, we proceeded to study *Mishna* [1] in the other room with Mr. Yehezkel. He took care of my education when I moved to a higher grade at the age of six. Finally, we finished at around thirteen or fourteen with Mr. Henoch Danzinger who used to teach us *Gemara* [2] in higher grades and guided us through deeper studies of *Talmud* [3], *Tosafot* [4], and of course Rashi [5] I also studied with Rabbi Izyk, my personal teacher, who prepared me and two other boys for *Yeshiva* [6] entrance exams. I progressed steadily and smoothly, I wanted to continue my education in the *Yeshiva* in Lublin. After taking exams, I was actually accepted there, to my great joy, but I was not able to even start my studies there. The war broke out and changed my plans. Many years after, I would tell our guide about it in Poland and he would show his true respect: "I know that only the most intelligent and promising students were accepted there. I heard how much they had to learn by heart from the most difficult parts of *Mishna* to go through the selection." My expectations and dreams about studying in the *Yeshiva* could not come true. The process of my religious education was brutally quenched in the middle, despite its positive and promising character. The Nazi invasion changed everything in my life, turning it upside down. Nevertheless, I am certain this period of time shaped my character, and its fruits helped me numerous times later in life.

The images of me as a young, learning boy have remained very deep inside me. These beautiful memories at the same time bring so much pain.

---

1   *Mishna*, Hebrew, "repetition," a major work of Rabbinic writings throughout the history; a source and tool for judgment, presenting the debate on the matter, in this way presenting the practice of the rules from the Bible

2   *Gemara*, Hebrew, "learning by tradition", the part of *Talmud* containing rabbinical commentaries and analysis of *Mishna*, which presents examples for discussion; the basis for codes of rabbinic law

3   *Talmud*, Hebrew, a record of rabbinic discussion referring to Jewish law, history and customs

4   *Tosafot*, Hebrew, "additions" medieval commentaries on the *Talmud*, written on the margin, presenting discussions over particular issues

5   Rashi, acronym of Rabbi Shlomo Yitzhaki, (1040 – 1105), a rabbi of France, known for his first comprehensive commentary on the *Talmud* written in the middle of it, praised for his ability to present the meaning in a clear and easily understood way

6   *Yeshiva*, Hebrew "sitting," a religious school teaching classical Judaism, *Torah*, *Talmud* and Rabbinic literature to older boys

They carry with them a heavy load of sorrow of what came so suddenly and brutally to this peaceful existence - death. Each recollection is marked with yearning for the murdered and lost forever world. I can only guess what happened to all my school friends and my teachers when the Nazi built the ghetto in Szczekociny and closed there all the Jews from my *shtetl* before they took them to Treblinka[1].

So many years have passed and to my surprise, I still can remember so many details! First of all, Mr. Litvak used to carry with him a small stick with twigs, which he would use to punish those who misbehaved. In those days corporal punishment was often practiced, and teachers had parental acceptance for that way of teaching their children discipline. Yet, I don't recall him using it; we knew our limits. The stick served more as a reminder to us of what could happen and how we should behave. Then, Mr. Yehezkel, had only one leg and used a crutch, which didn't seem to trouble him much. He used to walk so fast that he would reach all the places more quickly than we did, even though we were walking on two legs. Nobody could outwalk him. He was tall and handsome, and his face was always smiling. Mr. Dancinger was a true scholar; his method of teaching *Talmud* was smooth and peaceful, like a melody. The atmosphere was pleasant, and our studying easier and more effective also thanks to the Jewish jokes and funny stories that he told us. Thanks to his methods, we did not find learning difficult or boring. Instead, it was a smooth and pleasant journey through queries we had to solve from our holy books, until we reached the solution.

Mr. Litvak actually used to teach most of the town's youngest boys and we all loved him, since he was a not only truly talented and skillful but also a kind and noble man, truly devoted to children. I remember he would take us to the houses of women right after they gave birth to their babies; at that time, childbirth took place at home with the help of a midwife. We used

---

1   Treblinka: Nazi German extermination camp in the central Poland, where around 850,000 people were killed between July 1942 and October 1943, including Jewish communities from Szczekociny and Wodzislaw. The camp was destroyed and closed after the revolt during which a small number of prisoners managed to escape

to sing there *"Shema Israel"* [1] and *"HaMalach Hagoel"* [2]. We all used to come back to school with bags of sweets and all kinds of other goods that we received for our praying at homes that we visited. It continued until the ceremony of *Brit Milah* [3], i.e. until the eighth day after the birth of boys. It used to take place almost once every month, and we all liked it and had true fun.

We owe Mr. Litvak a lot. I remember Mr. Yehezkel praising us for what we knew when we came to his classes; it was nobody else's but Mr. Litvak's merit. Mr. Danzinger, on the other hand, was one of the best teachers for higher grades. At the age of ten I started a higher level of studying, i.e. the Five Books of Moses, Books of Prophets, and various interpretations. We were reading the original *Book of Esther* for *Purim*, and despite my young age I did not have any difficulties with understanding it. Thanks to the intensive education and wonderful skills of my teacher, after a short period of time, I was able to understand everything in Hebrew. Mr. Danzinger was a wise and demanding educator. He used to bring the most difficult parts from different *Talmud* tractates to challenge our thinking. "Why are we studying only the fragments and not whole writings?" children would ask him. He would look at us with a smile and say: "Children! You need to be independent. If you study with me the most difficult sections, you will be able to continue yourselves at home." He was right. I was truly devoted to my religious education, and studying the Bible used to bring me a lot of satisfaction and happiness.

Though I was given only fifteen years to live in Szczekociny, all my memories until the end are pleasant. What a boy my age could need more? Also, I am far from exaggerating when I say we, people in my *shtetl*, lived like one family. I remember we all tried to support each other as much as we could. Szczekociny had a bank with organized help for the poor. People

---

1   *Shema Israel*, Hebrew, "Hear, o Israel," the most important prayer in Judaism, and it is a religious commandment to recite it twice a day

2   *HaMalach Hagoel*, a prayer from Genesis 48:16, usually said by children at night before going to sleep; May the angel who has delivered me from all harm bless these lads

3   *Brit Milah*, Hebrew, a religious ceremony to welcome Jewish boys into a covenant between God and the Children of Israel through ritual circumcision performed on the eighth day

could borrow money whenever they needed it and, obviously, there was no interest imposed on the loans. I remember my dear father trying actively to help young people. As a matchmaker, he would first of all put the right people together. Then, instead of lending them money, which he obviously did not regard as wrong, he would rather help them open a shop to make them start a real life where they could make their own living. At the same time, he approved of charity, but he himself preferred an active way of helping young people. We always tried to help one another. I remember once a house belonging to a Jewish family was burnt. It was natural they would come and live with us until their own place was repaired. In the town prevailed positive attitudes, willingness to help and to support one another.

Obviously there were small clashes, as in all families, but people knew one another and, on the whole, cared about preserving a good atmosphere. I myself do not remember anything that I could call anti-Semitism, try as I may. Sometimes some incidents would start, usually out of jealousy, but there never was any real hate. Some Christians would call us Jews Moshek, whenever they did not know our names. Here and there one could hear "Moshek! Come over here, I have business to make with you!" It may have been slightly patronizing as such, but nobody felt offended and nobody had bad intentions. We needed them, they needed us, and we all realized that.

Both sides depended on each other to a certain extent; Christians used to say that we, Jews, rolled the wheel of business in the town, and that they were better off thanks to us. Some would envy us our better material situation, but it wasn't very serious. Jews generally tried not to show off with their financial status.

Many Christians worked for Jews at that time. Many young Christian girls took care of children, whereas adults helped in houses, especially during *Shabbat* and other holidays, performing certain duties that our *Halacha*[1] restricted. They would warm the house with fire on cold days and put the lights on when the dark was coming. We had a married couple living with us downstairs. They were Christians who would work for us, and we gave

---

1   *Halacha*, from the Hebrew derivative meaning "to walk" Jewish Religious Law, including rules from the Bible, rabbinic laws and customs and traditions specifying the Jewish religious and everyday life

them a place to live in. During the years they, as many others in similar circumstances, learned all our rules, and we did not have to tell them anything or ask them to do certain things; they knew themselves what was necessary. Jewish mothers, who were helped with their children by Gentile girls, did not have to worry at all about *Kashrut*; the girls also knew what food was allowed and how to serve it. They brought Jewish children up according to our Jewish tradition. Some of them would even say our prayer, *Mode Ani* in the morning with the children. It was common to see a Christian girl surrounded with Jewish children while all of them said together:

"I gratefully thank you, oh, living and eternal King,

for You have returned my soul within me

with compassion abundant is Your faithfulness!"

On the other hand, I remember visiting my Gentile friend, a chief policeman's daughter. We used to help each other with homework, and I used to study with her at times in her house, sometimes in the evening after school, sometimes in the morning before. During one of these early visits I saw my friend kneel down to the cross hanging on the wall and say a little prayer that unfortunately I could never remember again. I never saw anything like that before, and I watched this scene with true interest. Her father was at that time sitting at the table with breakfast and also saying some words of praying; I guessed it must have been their blessings of food. I thought then that their religion helped them to be good to one another.

Christian helpers also knew all types of Jewish blessings for food before and after eating. Many of them learned to speak Yiddish too. I think on the whole they were happy to live with us Jews. When Christmas or Easter was coming, we, as well as many other families, would present our Christian workers with special food and better clothes. My mother used to bake special, big *Challah* for them. In this way, we wanted to express our gratitude for their hard work and make them feel appreciated during that special time.

Now I am going back with all these experiences deep inside me; back to the place that I could not think calmly of for all those years. What will I find in my Szczekociny? Will there be any Jews living there? What will the atmosphere be there now, after the war? Did anybody come back, or the rumors after the war advising Jews not to were right? Will I see my house? How will I react?

The plane is landing. The nine-hour journey is finished, and I am growing apprehensive and tense. It is good my family is with me; they give me courage to face what is happening. Fifty-nine years after I was marched in freezing cold from my last place here, Auschwitz, in my striped, worn out uniform and wooden shoes, I am back. I know most of those survivors who came back regretted their decision later. They talked about witnessing cold emptiness after seeing the destroyed and irreversibly lost world. They felt a stifled, mute cry in the walls, and in the stones that witnessed the tragedy of the Jewish nation. They spoke of the pain they experienced returning to the places they remembered so well, in a hope they would touch again what they missed so much. Instead, they experienced bitter disappointment and had to realize, there is no coming back.

Am I going to face the same suffering? Soon I will find out. We have reached the place, Warsaw, Poland. My heart beats fast while I am going out of the plane to meet the old and new, the known and unknown.

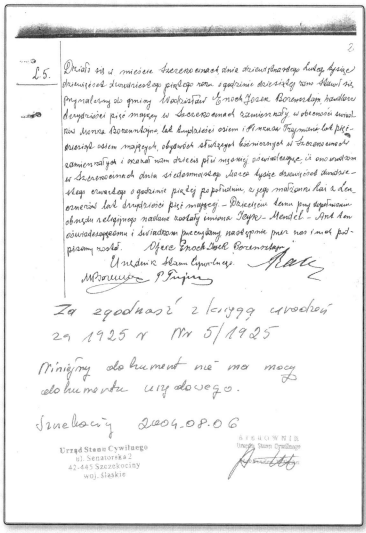

Trans. A. Piskiewicz: The certificate of birth of Izyk Mendel Bornstein obtained at the Municipality of Szczekociny in 2004

It happened in the town of Szczekociny on February 19th, 1925 at 10:00 a.m. There came Enoch Josek Borensztajn, a tradesman aged thirty five, belonging to the municipality of Wodzislaw and living in Szczekociny, accompanied by the witnesses: Moszek Borensztajn, aged thirty eight and Pinkas Trajman, aged fifty eight, both Szczekociny synagogue servants, and he showed us a male child claiming it was born in Szczekociny on March 17th, 1924 at 05:00 p.m. from his wife Laia from Lenczners, aged thirty five. Having performed religious rituals, the boy was named Icyk Mendel. The document was read to the witnesses and signed by us and them.

The father, Enoch Josek Borensztajn

The Civil Office Worker

THREE

I am looking around carefully. Never was I in Warsaw before, but I already notice how much the country has changed, how modern it has become. I hear the language. I haven't used it since I left, but I realize it sounds very familiar. I am able to catch some words, though I don't feel I can talk myself. Our guide, Tomasz Kuberczyk, speaks Hebrew and Yiddish, which is a great advantage. We get into the car and set off on our destination.

From the very beginning, we decide not to enter any of the Nazi camps so it will not make my comeback more difficult for me. According to the schedule, we are heading now for Krakow with a short stop in Kielce on the way, where some of my family used to live before the war. Then we are supposed to go to Szczekociny and Wodzislaw. I try to be calm, but inside I cannot contain my excitement.

It rains heavily all the way. I had forgotten how torrential and persistent rains in Poland could be. Thanks to the rain, however, it is very green. Ahead of us, we have a five-hour drive, with a stop in Kielce. Slowly, I start to relax a little. I watch the landscape through the window and share my recollections with my excited family.

Quite a few people from my closest family lived in Kielce before the war. My father's sister, Rachel, moved there with her husband, Jacob Goldblum. My mother's only sister, Hinda, followed her husband to Kielce too, after she got married to Zelig Silberstain. When my elder siblings, my brother Chaim Schlomo and my sister Sara Akresz got married, they also decided to start their new lives in this city. They could make a better living there.

Shlomo quickly learned a profession. He decided he would sour the leather of shoes. He cut leather and produced uppers to the shoes, and was successful in his job indeed. He used to make a lot of money out of this occupation. A few times a year, usually during High Holidays time, he would visit us in the family house. I remember him as a handsome, young man; for me he looked like a young, elegant prince, always dressed in magnificent suits. When he would come home, he used to make all the children very happy by bringing us candy, chocolates, different kind of nuts, and also shoes. He made them for us, according to our sizes, both boots for winter and sandals for summer. Sara's husband, Kalman Samburski, worked for his father in his candy factory. She could not complain about her material status either; the factory was truly prosperous, and they led a happy, calm life. Also their visits were very sweet for us, as they would bring with them candy from the factory, and we tasted different kinds of sweets that we did not have every day. As children, we always looked forward to the visits of our elder siblings. They never forgot about their younger brothers and sisters and made these times true holidays for us.

I myself had never been to Kielce before. When I was a child, people did not travel a lot; there were not many means of transportation. The most popular way was a wagon with horses. It was very rare that we moved outside our *shtetl*, but when we did, it was usually for school, important family visits, or to bring goods for the shop. My father would travel once a week to Lodz to bring different materials for tailors. He had a shop with textiles.

After the war I heard about the pogrom that took place in Kielce. Almost forty Jews died at hands of Poles, because of the quickly spreading rumor of blood libel. Quite a lot of Poles believed that we Jews used human blood in our religious rituals, and that child blood was allegedly most precious. In 1946 a boy left his family home without his parents' knowledge and was looked for. Jewish neighbors were accused of having detained him. Rumors spread quickly and riots resulted. The crowd of people broke into the house where allegedly the boy was kept. There were fights that involved also the Police and, before it turned out that the story was not true, innocent people were murdered. Kielce was not unique in this, unfortunately. The atmosphere right after the war was openly anti-Semitic in the majority of places. The six years of war and the accompanying Nazi propaganda seemingly reached a fertile ground, and many Poles became hostile and aggressive. Many believed various myths spread about Jews, which resulted in numerous tragedies.

Nowadays, Kielce is a city of slightly over two hundred thousand people. Before the war, around twenty-five thousand Jews used to live here, which made almost one-fourth of the whole population out of the approximate number of eighty thousand. The city used to be a meaningful Jewish community in Poland. Most of its members were, however, executed on the spot, in the labor camp that was created here or taken to Treblinka, Auschwitz, and Buchenwald and murdered in those camps. What happened to my family from this city? How did my dear brother and sister die? I was never to find out.

My uncle was the owner of a bakery in Kielce, where he also lived with his family, and a warehouse, where they stored flour. The bakery was named after the brother, Elash Goldblum; it was a family business. I remember my father used to send many letters to 10 Staszica Street; this is the only address I remember from this city. After some walking in the town, we reach the street. I become more disillusioned with each step, however. Everything seems to have been renovated; there are new shops stretching around everywhere. When number ten lies in front of us, to my disappointment, there are new buildings standing there. This seems natural, after such a long time, I suppose.

Tomasz suggests going inside the yard. There, we meet an elderly woman, and as I recall, Tomasz asks her questions, trying to find out any information of this place. She confirms there used to be a bakery here, and to our surprise, she says, "It still used to work many years after the war. They closed it only five years ago." My heart starts beating faster. We see some old buildings behind, and she confirms our expectations! This is the old bakery of my uncle! It is still standing, in quite a good condition, though it is locked by the government. I am truly touched. I didn't have a chance to see the place while it was operating and prospering; I can only imagine what it used to be like. In my mind's eye, I see the hectic, simple life: fresh loaves of bread, their smell, queues of people coming to buy them, cheerful conversations of my uncles working hard. I stand there a while looking at the walls and its windows that seem to me as hollowed eyes. If only they could talk! If only they could tell me what happened here! Instead, there is deathly silence.

Nevertheless, the material touch of the past encourages me a little and adds some strength.

In Krakow, my memories of the pre-war Jewish Poland are revived even more. Kazimierz, the Jewish district, is hardly destroyed. Renovated, its buildings are mostly changed into hotels and restaurants, commercial in its atmosphere, but still one can feel the Jewish spirit in the air. We visit numerous synagogues, all quite well-preserved.

We enter Remuh Synagogue. A guard, Mr. Liban, happens to be an ex-prisoner of Plaszow. He has a book on the table in front of him, Ich, Oskar Schindler. He sees us looking at it. "I was taken to Gross-Rosen from Plaszow," he says, "and from Gross-Rosen I was saved by Schindler himself." I tell him that I was a prisoner in Plaszow too. Liban mentions some names he remembers, Muller and Amon Gett, two main commanders from the camp. I also know them. Listening to him talking to Tomasz, our translator, I am too excited to wait for the translation. I can understand everything. I turn to Mr. Liban and ask him in Polish, "Do you remember Commandant Jon?" He looks at me but does not seem to recall that name at all. I, however, remember him very well. I will never forget.

It was in Plaszow Gulag II, in the summer of 1943. Every now and then Nazis used to pick out a group of fifty or sixty of prisoners from among us. They were walked to an unknown location and never came back. It seemed a random choice. The Nazis would simply come and carelessly point: "You, you, and you." I did not know why or where they were taken, until one day I found myself among those selected. The head of the camp, Herr Jon, selected this time around two hundred of us. Was it due to the fact it was *Yom Kippur*, our holiest festival? The date could not escape our attention; the peak of their cruelties surprisingly tended to coincide with our religious main holidays. They arranged us in fours and led us to meet our destiny. We were marched as soldiers: "Right, left, right, left!" The faces of all of us betrayed fear, all contorted in pain. I was also scared, and I had no idea what they were going to do with me and with all of us marching to their rule. I could not help the growing premonition that I may not come back anymore.

Finally, we reached the huge pit on a small hill, distant from the sounds of working machines and yelling Nazis. On the side, we spotted two digging tractors. The commandant sat at a small table, sipping his whiskey calmly, his weapon next to him. He told us to line up along the edge with our backs to him, I found myself in the middle. At that moment we were hit with the obvious truth. Now we knew where all the others had been disappearing. There was no coming back from where they had been taken, and now we were joining them. Our lives had come to an end, without warning, without preparation. We were all panicked, lost and crying, overwhelmed with fear and sorrow, we were standing there helplessly shaking with overwhelming terror, facing a certain death. Thoughts were racing through my head. My heart was beating like crazy. There were so many things I hadn't managed to do! What about my parents, my brother? I was not ready to die yet! Who was? It couldn't be helped. It had happened so quickly, and we had no choice. Through those short seconds, which felt like hours, I managed to embrace my whole life, to experience the flood of not only my most profound, and painful emotions, but also to see and feel inside me everything I had experienced so far. In such a short time, when I was paralyzed with fear, I managed to think of all my family, of Szczekociny, of everything precious to me that I was about to lose forever.

At last the moment came. The commandant stood up, drank his last sip from the glass, saluted "Heil Hitler!" and picked up his machine gun. This was the time everything around stopped for me. It was as if the world froze and I froze with it as well. "Goodbye, my life!" I cried inside my body. A moment later, exposed to a rain of sharp shots, we were riddled with bullets.

The yelling that was born inside us and pierced the indifferent air was as sharp as the bullets piercing our bodies. Soon I was inside the pit, being hit by the others' limbs, which were moving in uncontrolled convulses of death. I realized I had been pushed. I felt it was somebody's hands that pushed me decisively and strongly inside, but I did not focus on it as I was shocked and petrified. I saw blood on my body and knew I had died. I was dead. I lay there for a whole eternity. Next, I felt hands on my body and realized that I was being pulled out. Where am I? I wondered. Who are those faces looking at me in disbelief? Is this a regular experience after death?

Still shocked and insecure, I could not stand on my feet, but I made all the efforts and tried hard to understand what had happened. The people who pulled me out of the pit turned out to be the special commando unit, whose task was to complete the mission of commanders. They were called

Totenkommando, I found out later. I slowly tried to grasp their words and make some sense of them. They had arrived at the place approximately twenty minutes after the shooting and started their job. They were stretching the dead bodies arranging them like sardines: head to feet, feet to head. Before putting them on fire, they were lavishly pouring gasoline over them, which helped to keep the smell down and quickened the process of destroying the bodies. After that, they covered them with a level of ground. In this way, the pit was soon ready for the next action. I felt I was growing more and more sick and feeble.

That day the Tottenkommando arrived as usual and silently went on to perform their gloomy tasks: a peculiar funeral according to Nazi rules. Paradoxically, the commando were chosen from among the Jewish prisoners as well. They, however, remained unaware of the sad fact that they too were sentenced to death. With all the knowledge they had of what was happening, the Tottencommando units were replaced with new prisoners every time the Nazis decided it would be too dangerous to continue with them. That day, they for the first time, they experienced something new. They were shocked to see one of the bodies, covered with blood, still moving although it had been so long since the shooting had taken place. I myself had no idea how much time I spent there; it could have been a few minutes, it could have been ages, for I had been certain I was dead. The Totenkommando didn't not know what to do with me. I presume they were scared too, and thinking hard about which decision would protect them from any repercussions. In the camp, it was very easy to attract anger and dissatisfaction of the Nazis, which could also easily end with losing your life. Finally, the Tottencommando decided to take me to the nearby women's camp, where they were sewing white uniforms for Nazis to prevent them from being spotted during winter days. They cleaned the blood from me and dressed in one of the white pieces of clothing. In those symbolic clothes, which intensified the incomprehensible situation of my peculiar resurrection, they decided to take me to the commander to get a further decision.

Once my senses started to work again, I became petrified at their decision. If I wasn't killed before, I will be killed now, I thought. After a few minutes I was facing the man, who moments before, was shooting at me. I was not only supposed to be dead sharing the fate of the other selected; I was also a witness to what had been taking place there. Was there any other destiny for me but death? The commandant looked at me carefully, surprised at what he was told and I began to shrink under his emotionless eyes. That short moment was filled with so many feelings inside my weak heart; I think if it had lasted any second later, I would have passed out. He finally said, "OK, since he survived in such a way, give him a day off, and tomorrow let him continue. Take him back to the camp."

I was coming back slowly, completely stunned. The verdict was proclaimed in my favor. Even now I cannot understand it; it is completely beyond any comprehension. I was saved a few times that day. None of the bullets he fired touched me. The blood on my body came from the bodies of my friends; all of whom, obviously, died on the spot. I was recognized alive by the commando unit; thanks to the fact I had not fainted completely and was moving, which made them pull me out. The remorseless Nazi, who without a twinge of conscience was carrying on cruel executions day by day, not only granted me life instead of finishing and correcting this strange mistake, which must have been nothing else for him, but he also allowed me a day of rest! He could have killed me on the spot; he could have left me for another execution. Can anybody understand it?

I have no idea if such thing had ever happened before or after; I still cannot fathom it. I keep wondering whose hands I felt on my body pushing me inside the pit. One may wonder: was it a coincidence or destiny? For me it was the first sign, which I understood only later. I was literally pulled out of Death's arms, which were so close, trying to embrace me, together with my other comrades.

Then the date hit me again. *Yom Kippur.* I looked at myself, dressed in white clothes, precisely according to our tradition. I tried to embrace all that had happened in the last few hours. God, have you just sealed me in the Book of Life? Will I survive the war? Is this a message? I recalled all the *Yom Kippur* festivals in Szczekociny, where people wearing white clothes used to make me think of angels. Finally, I could release all the emotions. I started crying, letting out all the tension, pressure, and fear. I wished there was anybody next to me to help me go through it. I so much wished I were not alone.

Three

A day later I went back to my regular camp life, with all its activities and duties, with regular humiliation and fear inflicted by our tormentors. Inside, however, I was changed forever.

"Amon Gett," says Mr. Liban in the Remuh synagogue, bringing me back to reality, when I finish telling my story. "He was the one shooting."

Yes, I remembered that he was one of the top important figures there, and it could have been him shooting at us once we were selected by Jon. I was so shocked and petrified at that time that I could not be sure. "I know it, because I was in the bunker at those moments," the guard adds.

Having prayed in Remuh Synagogue, I decide to say *kaddish*[1] in its cemetery for my beloved family, who perished in the Holocaust. It is a very difficult and at the same time a truly special and symbolic moment, bearing in mind the place and circumstances. We stand at Rabbi Moses' grave[2], the most important place in this cemetery. My voice keeps breaking down; it is hard to speak the names of my lost parents, brothers, and sisters. For a long time I stand silent, trying to swallow that pain tightening my throat and making me unable to utter any word. No matter how hard I try, I cannot overcome it. Instead, there are tears and my trembling, weak voice. I am standing there, feeling so miserable; me, the sole survivor of the nine people in my family, of all my siblings, parents, numerous uncles and aunts. What happened to your bodies? Where are your ashes? What did they do to all of you? Why? What wrong had we done? My heart is asking again the old, painful questions. Would the answers bring me any comfort? Would I feel calmer knowing? I cannot be sure of that.

I have no possibility to visit the graves of my closest family, unlike all other people around the world, regardless of their religion. My family has only a symbolic grave, which is the Polish land, soaked with our blood, ashes, and

1   *Kaddish*, Arameic: "holy", Jewish prayer of magnification and sanctification of God's name, often used to refer specifically to "mourners' *kaddish*", as here, recited after the death and at each death anniversary, obliging the relatives of the dead to say this prayer in accordance with the rules

2   Rabbi Moses Isserles, a scholar and philosopher, whose father, Israel Isserles Auerbach founded the synagogue, which was named Remuh to honor Rabbi Moses. Each year, thousands of Jews reach his grave to pray, writing notes with their requests

tears. Instead, I say prayers for them in one of the oldest Jewish cemeteries in Poland. Surrounded with my dear children's supportive and protective arms, I unite with the spirits of my perished family.

We continue our visits to Kazimierz synagogues. At the entrance to Wysoka, to our regret, it turns out it is closed. Here, however, another significant event takes place. We see an elderly woman standing next to the entrance, who seems to be clearly disappointed. "My father used to be a manager of this synagogue," she tells us. "I wanted to come inside and they wouldn't let me in," she complains. Having checked the situation, it turns out a private workshop is being built inside. We cannot enter at the moment. We, however, continue our conversation with the woman. Her name is Gienia Manor. To my surprise, it turns out she is also a Plaszow survivor, another that I meet during this short time. "I came here with a group of students from Jerusalem," she explains. "They take me with them every year as a witness, and I tell them the story of my survival." We spend some time talking to each other and sharing our experiences, taking the opportunity of such an unexpected meeting.

There, in Krakow I make the decision: "I want to go to Plaszow and Auschwitz too. I want to see these places again." My family is worried about my condition and how I will react. "I will manage." I convince them. Obviously I feel fear inside, but I know it can also be the last time I have this opportunity. I want to show my family the places where I was exposed to the greatest suffering in my life, which changed me forever. I suddenly feel I want to face the past, to see what there is now, if they look the same, if there are any traces, any remains of the times before. The courage rising inside slowly smothers my apprehension. I am ready.

FOUR

I arrived in Plaszow Gulag I in October of 1942 as a result of a trap prepared for us Jewish men by Nazis. I was in Zarnowiec at that time, hiding with my younger brother, Jacob Hersh (Zvi), at my uncle's shelter. Abraham Yishaya Lenczner, my mother's brother, was hiding at a Polish family's shelter. Zarnowiec was a village located approximately twenty kilometers from Szczekociny. My uncle had been staying there already for a while when we finally joined him, following the decision of my dear father.

Before, we had stayed with my parents, my brother and two sisters in the ghetto of Wodzislaw, the family town of my father. Right before the High Holidays of September 1942, however, everything started to change dramatically. Around that time, my father, who was appreciated in the community, brought the information from the Jewish community that something bad was going to happen soon. Nazis were said to have been planning something much more serious than what had happened so far been aimed at us Jews. Yet, we were not told any details. Here and there some news was smuggled to the closed world in which we lived. It was always saddening and depriving us of hopes; news of cruelty that people experienced from the invaders. Did my father know more and simply want to save us from the scary truth, protecting his family? I will never know this.

Now, though deeply saddened, my father remained stable and acted immediately, with no second thoughts. He called for Jacob and me and said, "I order you to immediately leave the house and go through the fields to your uncle. Stay there and save yourselves."

For a short moment, there was an absolute silence. We remained speechless, shocked at what we had just heard. "What is going happen to you should also happen to us," I said finally with conviction, though in a trembling voice. "We cannot separate!" I added desperately. Jacob was petrified, as he looked helplessly at us. "The Poles will not agree." I was desperately clutching at straws, trying to convince my father to change his decision. "It will be a much higher risk now for them to hide three Jews instead of one!" I hoped that my father would realize that those Poles who were hiding my uncle would not agree to take two other men, which would put them in danger and thus would be no shelter for us. I meant it, but first of all I did not want to separate from my family. It was such an uncertain time, we all dreaded for our lives, and lived in constant apprehension. Being together with the family soothed our apprehension a little.

My father, however, was well-prepared for his mission. He was deeply convinced the family sheltering my uncle would not refuse, especially since we would pay for it and my dear uncle would help us as well. "I know Abraham. I know he will accept you there. We are a family and should support each other, especially in hard times. Everything is already arranged," my father stated firmly. I looked at my mother, trying to get her support. She was making all the efforts to stay stable, but her face betrayed deep suffering and fear. Even though, I knew this was a unanimous decision, and she would not question anything my father stated.

We cried despairingly with Jacob. Devastated, at all costs we were trying to stay with all the family. No tears or protests could change my father's decision, however. "You are obliged to respect the commandments. I am your father, and you have to listen to me. That's it. You need to go!"

He gave us the address and the hats that were typically worn by Polish Christian men at that time. We were to pretend we were regular peasants, shepherds. My fifteen-year-old brother and me, two-and-a-half-years older at that time, reluctantly and with broken hearts left our family. We had no other choice. I knew my father was trying to save us. Our leaving must have been the same difficulty for him. Nevertheless, this knowledge did not bring me any comfort. It was so tough to leave them all there, waiting for Germans to attack.

It was one of the most dramatic moments I came to experience during that difficult period of the war. Maybe deep inside, without realizing it, I knew that I would never see them again.

We succeeded in leaving the ghetto and set off on our sad journey. We kept walking silently. We were devastated and feared for both what we had left behind and the unknown ahead of us. We held sticks and kept off the main roads, walking through the fields, just like our father had told us. I tried to give my younger brother some confidence, but inside I felt the same sadness and insecurity. What if they did not agree? What would we do then? Where would we go? I dreaded to think. Each step we were further from our family, more and more insecure, and our hearts heavier. In the distance we saw local villages, but we kept away from all houses. It would be too risky for us had we been caught. Jews were not allowed to be walking freely. Finally, after some hours of wandering, we arrived at where my uncle was staying. The rich Polish family had quite a lot of land and a big farm. There was always something to do there, especially in the autumn days of harvesting the crops. The plan was that we would help them in their everyday farm duties. Fortunately for us, and to our great relief, the hosts agreed to give us shelter. Thus, we joined our uncle, which gave us somewhat of a feeling of comfort and safety, even though, we could not stop thinking about our parents and siblings. Were they still well, where we left them? What bad things were the Nazis planning? Our fear for them did not let us stay calm.

We lived in hiding slightly over the month. In late October, our circumstances began to change. There came an order to gather all young Jewish men, aged from seventeen to thirty, in a specified place. Though my brother was not even sixteen at that time, we both shared a strong conviction that we were not going to separate anymore. My uncle, was over thirty, so he could stay where he was. We were apprehensive and did not know what that order meant, but we could not risk it. If the Nazis found us later in our shelter, both we and our hosts could die. We hoped all would finish well for everyone. We said good bye and left again.

It was still before sunset. We came at the place and joined others, all insecure alike. Guarded by Nazi and Polish officers, we marched, truly scared and uncertain of what would happen next. They were leading us to an unknown destiny. Suddenly, I saw a familiar face, and after a closer examination, I recognized one of the Polish officers as the father of one of my schoolmates. It was his daughter that used to go to the same class with me; we used to do homework together at her house. I felt more confident and decided to take a risk. I approached him and asked, "Where are they taking us? What is going on?" I don't know if he recognized me. He looked around carefully, for he must have felt as insecure as we did, and replied quietly, "You are going to spend the night in prison. Tomorrow morning you are going to be transferred to Miechow. There are no more Jews there. You are going to load their furniture and possessions onto the trucks."

We were confused and scared at this information. What did he mean by the ominous statement: "There are no more Jews there"? What did they do to them? What was going to be with us? We didn't want to leave another place that we had become to know and separate with no information from the family. However, what else could we do? There was no going back now.

In the morning we were gathered and told to climb onto trucks. It was all done in a cold-hearted rush from the Germans. We had not recovered yet after the separation with our family and again we were thrown into the whirl of events. The fact that I was with Jacob definitely gave both of us some courage and comfort in these fearful circumstances. I did not suspect it that that would come to an end so quickly and brutally. We were sitting together quietly awaiting our journey. And then, all of a sudden, things changed dramatically in a few seconds. One of the Nazis who came to close the door looked at my brother, and dragged him off the truck. "You are too young! Get down!" he cried angrily, without paying any attention to our cries. It happened so quickly that I was not even given a chance to say good bye properly to him. I felt the rest of the pieces of my world fell completely apart. I looked painfully at Jacob who had been forced to leave and ordered him quickly to go back from where we had come, to rejoin our uncle Abraham. "You will be safe with him. When it is possible, I will contact you" I told him through my tears. He nodded his head, still in shock and left uncertainly, hastened by the Nazis. At the time, it seemed the worst thing that could happen to us. Now our family was spread around, lonely and without news from one another. I was overwhelmed with pain and felt I could not carry more on my shoulders. I had to worry about myself, about Jacob, about my parents and sisters in Wodzislaw and Sara and Schlomo in Kielce.

Although I couldn't know it at that time, it was the last time I saw my dear brother.

On the truck without him, I felt completely abandoned. Each kilometer was taking me further from the world I used to know. I was crammed in the truck with strangers. Their faces betrayed the feelings of apprehension and fear. I must have looked the same. We all had left everyone and everything behind. Would I be able to come back? Did Jacob find his way back home safely? What was happening with my parents and sisters? How were my siblings managing in Kielce? The questions were filling my head, coming back over and over again. Would the day ever come when we would all meet again in our family home in Szczekociny? In my mind's eye I saw us reunited telling each other what we went through, supporting and comforting each other. Maybe it would not last long. Maybe after a few more weeks the war would be over. I recalled the army from Szczekociny. Poland would not surrender, certainly, but we had to believe this nightmare would soon come to an end.

The truck finally stopped, and my thinking came to an end with the yelling ordering us to go out. The journey did not take much more than an hour. We were led into the empty building. It was true there were no more Jews, apparently, but there was no more furniture either. Was it a trap? They had lied to us! There was no work to do! What now? There were long, anxious moments before things started to become clear. In the afternoon we were gathered again and taken to the railway station. Nazis started to cram us into wooden cattle-trucks, as if we were animals. They screamed all the time, while we tried desperately not to make them angrier and to follow their commands. We all felt scared and lost.

Where were they taking us? What transport was this? They shoved hundreds of us into one truck with a small window and locked the door. It was dark and stuffy; we stood tight to each other, unable to move. After a few minutes, we were all striving to fill our lungs with at least one breath of fresh air - futile attempts, since the small and cramped space could not by any chance provide it. We were all breathing in the air that had already gone through the lungs of others. We all were fighting with ourselves to endure a little more. We tried hard not to give up and start screaming. I myself kept looking at the tiny window, and trying to smother the strong instinct to rush to it and get some air, through the others, pushing them all aside to make way for myself. We stood virtually with no space from ourselves, touching each other with all our bodies. It was not only physical, but also a psychological violation of our freedom and safety, done with cruel premeditation.

Four

Eventually, after what could not have been more than an hour but for us seemed the whole eternity, the train stopped. Open the door! We all begged and moaned quietly inside our agonized bodies. Air! Light! Finally! We literally slumped to the ground, before we were hastened by the Nazi's yelling, which was soothed with the blast of fresh air that pleasantly hit our anguished faces. We looked around with apprehension, gasping for the first breaths and drawing them greedily into our lungs. What a relief! We were marched from the railway station to the building concentration stretching nearby. When we reached the place, we saw simple barracks. It looked like a labor camp. We were in Plaszow, the district of Krakow.

From the very beginning they made us understand the harsh, severe conditions we were to expect there. The Jewish people who met us at the entrance rained heavy blows on us, accompanied by curses and swear words. I looked at the bands at their arms. They all said, "Capo." I was truly shocked by their behavior. "What are you doing? You are Jewish as well, just like us!" I could not suppress my indignation. In reply I got a cold order: "Do what I am telling you!" I was truly bewildered and did not know what to think of it. A closed area, Jewish men behaving the same as our enemies… what is happening? In the world I understood, this should not have been possible. Little did I know how many more times I would have to radically change my worldview.

They made us stand in a line and gave us a meal after this draining day. It was supposed to be a cabbage soup with two slices of dark bread. However, it did not resemble these at all. The liquid was tasteless, thin and watery, and the bread was incredibly hard. This was our new food, I realized. Once we had finished, they started to move us to our new accommodations. Our new home was a set of crude and cold cabins with a mattress per five people, dropped one next to another on the floor. We got some thin, ragged blankets, apparently to cover ourselves, again one for five of us. The night was falling, and we were ordered to go to sleep. No talking, no moving. They made us feel like prisoners. It was a terrible time. I was crowded among strangers, none of us knowing what would come or what to expect. Each of us must have been thinking about what we had left behind, our safe world, now destroyed and gone. I kept thinking about my younger brother, hoping he had found his way back and was safely hiding, and about the rest of my family, wondering what would become of them and if ever we would be able to see each other again. I was very tired, but I couldn't sleep well. I felt truly apprehensive and lost. It seemed only a few moments had passed since we were told to sleep when suddenly the lights went, and we heard someone yelling ordering us to get up immediately. Each cabin had an officer in charge, ex-criminals who had spent previous years in penitentiaries, we later found out. They had their own small rooms, where they sat observing us. Their task was to keep their eyes on us, taking care that we perform the orders immediately these are given. They "helped" and "motivated" us with their sticks raining down on our bodies and their cold yelling *"Schneller! Schneller!"*[1] I understood they expected us to stand upright and leave the cabin the moment they turned the electricity on.

Outside there were wooden shoes waiting for us. Each of us had to grab a pair and stand in groups of threes. They took our clothes and replaced them with camp uniforms: hats, striped shirts, and trousers and long coats. They looked more like pajamas or prisoner outfits. They were definitely depressing. We were made to practice taking our hats off and putting them on, until we did it the right way, like robots - all together, in unison.

They gave us metal bowls and cutlery. In the kitchen, located approximately two hundred feet from our barrack, we had our first breakfast: a small amount of porridge, two slices of bread, and black coffee. After this meal, we were lined in threes again and escorted by German and Ukrainian guards to work. They led us to a huge open land moving with Germans, engineers, tractors, and railways with wagons. We were given tools for digging, but we also had to work hard with our hands. We tilled the hard ground and shoveled the dirt. We had to load the wagons with sand and move them, as if we were horses, to a certain place where the wagon was turned over, and the sand was poured out. The group I was working with was responsible for relocating the rails. We had to carry them away, while Germans used screws and attached them together, creating a railway. We were told the plan was to build a railway station. After a whole day of tremendous work, we were escorted back to the camp, passing through a small building with a narrow passage, which served as an entrance gate to the workplace.

---

1   *Schneller*, German, "faster"

We were exhausted and starving, dreaming of something substantial to eat, adequate to the work we had done. An evening meal consisted again of two slices of hard bread, margarine, jam, and black coffee. Not only was the nutritional value really poor, the amount we received was scarce as well, definitely not for men our age and neither for the work we were performing. Right after dinner, we were rushed to take a shower. The German supervisor gave us soap and towels, and exactly five minutes to complete the task. He turned the tap on and off again right away, and by then, we were supposed to be back outside, where they gave us new clothes, still warm from disinfection. There were some who were more reluctant with showering. The Nazis were, however, very prompt to help them; they laid such people down on the floor, opened the taps and kept scrubbing the poor victims with metal brushes until death. Nothing would make them hesitate, stop, or show regret - neither the cries and screams of the oppressed, nor our fear lurking in our wide-open eyes. Petrified and shocked, we could not believe what we all saw happening openly in front of us. We stifled our emotions, swallowing the tears of fright deep into our stomachs. Any uncontrolled reaction could encourage them to help us share the fates of our poor comrades. Our horror was growing, as we understood how serious things had become.

The camp, we learned with time, was Plaszow Gulag I, whereas the name of the railway station was Muller Froitzheim. Muller was the name of the camp commander. He had a big dog and rode a horse. Around him, there was a young, very pretty Jewish boy he had chosen from the group, who lived with him. Muller took care of him, giving him good conditions. We couldn't help at times feeling jealousy inside our sad hearts, seeing him being allowed things forbidden to us that we could only dream of. Every now and then we saw the boy riding a horse, smiling with pleasure. Obviously, he was given much better food as well. However, none of us would have liked to be in his humiliating position.

Days came and went away, each new one resembling the one that passed before. Slowly, we grew accustomed to our new life with all the restrictions, orders, and prohibitions. It was not difficult or time-consuming to learn what was prohibited, since literally everything was forbidden. Cold yelling, whips, and sticks accompanying us wherever we moved were very helpful in the process of remembering. Once beaten by a fierce guard, we learned that we were not allowed to say a word during nights, unless we wished to face his visit with a stick again.

In the mornings, when leaving the barrack in a hurry, hastened with a whip and yelling, we actually never managed to find our own wooden clogs among the whole collection that we left inside each evening. We simply grabbed any two we could, taking care to do it quickly enough not to expose ourselves to the anger of the guard, which would result in tough beating. Later, if it happened that we took two of the same foot, we looked for each opportunity to change the mistaken shoes with other inmates, who did the same. We were slowly turning into robots, reacting only to the orders of our owners. We were hastened and rushed with each command, at times also treated with whips or sticks battering our bodies, growing thinner each day, reminding us we were only labor animals.

From the very beginning, they shaved our heads and took care not to let the hair regrow by shaving us deeply, with full force and precision, every few weeks. Apparently, it served hygienic reasons, yet it was a clear humiliation. Apart from the painful process itself, we no longer resembled human beings, all losing our dignity and individuality. The caps we had did not help at all, and on colder days we felt we were freezing. Also here, Nazis were violating our religious laws, which clearly specify the hair cutting processes[1]. With aching hearts, we humbly adjusted to their requirements; we all wanted to stay alive.

Each day was the same. We awakened at dawn, ate our portions of meager food, and were escorted to work. We marched silently to perform our daily chores, permanently scared and watchful. We toiled relentlessly, up to twelve-hour shifts, under German supervision, and at dusk we were taken back to the camp. We grew famished, and the meals we were provided left us even more hungry, slightly teasing our tightening stomachs. Hard work was depriving us of both strength and weight. Real food remained in the dreaming sphere. We carefully ate all the crumbs before we were rushed for a short shower and then a few hours of sleep. Actually, we were fortunate if

---

1   According to the Bible, shaving of the corners of the head and marring the corners of the beard is forbidden, and priests should not shave their heads

we were allowed to sleep. Since we were merely labor animals, apart from the daily toil, we were also forced to work most of the nights. Exhausted after long and difficult hours of daily shifts, weak due to malnutrition and constant fear, we were woken up in the middle of the night and taken to the arriving trains. They would bring from six to eight wagons loaded with black coal that looked like gravel, and we had to obviously unload it all. The cabin supervisor would come and look for volunteers; if there were none, he would pick people himself. We decided to go in turns so that everybody would take his share of the burden, which seemed the most honest thing. We would not have endured much longer had we gone each time. Having finished the night job, we were lucky if we managed to get some sleep. Soon the day came with its usual duties to perform.

One night, as before, we were awakened by the supervisor; the train had arrived. There were six people to unload the wagons, and I was among them. To my surprise and happiness, I discovered that one of the wagons was filled with freshly baked bread. I took advantage of it. While unloading it, I tried secretly to eat as much as possible until I felt full. I couldn't believe my luck, and I thanked God I had had to go that night. I decided to take some pieces with me to the camp. First of all, I knew such a present would not come again, so it would help to soothe the hunger later. Also, I felt I had to share with others in the camp too. I could not miss such opportunity, of that I was sure. I hid some pieces under my shirt and fastened them with the belt. I also tied a piece of rope to the lower part of my trousers and attached some portions there too, so that I would share with the hungry ones in the camp. I felt so happy about that and couldn't wait to give some of the treasure to my comrades. When I was passing through the narrow entrance passage, slightly apprehensive, but brave enough and self-controlled, I suddenly saw Muller's boy. One look from him, and it was clear he knew everything. For a moment I hoped it was nothing, that he would keep it for himself, for he was Jewish as I. He must have known my hunger and realized why I had done it. For this short moment when our eyes met, which seemed an eternity, I hoped shyly everything would be all right. Then I saw him entering the cabin.

Sadly, he informed to the guards in the passage of what I had done, and they reacted right away. They pulled me fiercely inside and threw me into a chair with my back to them. They took my pants off and started hitting me with the leash with all their power. I screamed and cried out loud; the pain was unbearable. Each of them was going to hit me five times, as they planned; altogether I was supposed to get twenty hits. At a certain moment, however, my body became so swollen that I could feel no more pain, and I became silent. I was on the verge of passing out. It worked in my favor, since they understood it differently. One of the torturers said, "Let's leave him; he is *kaput*" [1] They thought I had already died from the beating, so it was no use hitting me anymore. They dragged me outside and left me carelessly on the ground, as if I were a meaningless bag. I lay there for a moment unable to move, scared that they would see me and come back to finish their job. I felt truly lost. I knew I could face the same punishment coming back to the cabin, as I would break the rule and disturb the night silence. What to do? I couldn't decide. I was aching all over, both my body and my humiliated soul. I could not understand such cruelty for a few pieces of bread to a hungry, thin man. Neither could I grasp the behavior of Muller's boy. Why did he do it to me? Shouldn't he rather have protected and supported me? I was too naïve.

I asked all those questions as I crawled slowly to the cabin. I somehow managed to reach it, crying all the way from the pain, fear, and humiliation. However, I did not go inside; it was too risky. I spent the rest of the night sitting quietly at the wall. In the morning, I jumped quickly, joining the rest of the group going out to work. I was still aching all over, but at the same time, I was satisfied, as still some bread was left in my trousers, and I was able to give it to some hungry friends, which made me happy. Even though my body was swollen for over a week, I kept on working as usual to save my life.

Sometime after this event, while looking out of the window in our barrack, suddenly we noticed Muller and his boy. It was a regular day, still before sunset, so we could see clearly enough. The young boy was digging in the ground with a spade, and when finished, he put it aside and went inside. To our shock, we then saw Muller take his gun and shoot the boy whose body collapsed into the hole. We later understood he had been told to dig

---

1   *Kaput*, German, destroyed, broken; here, colloquial, dead or killed

his own grave. Why? What had happened? We couldn't understand; he was Muller's favorite! We quickly hid inside, getting away from the window, not to be seen. This event depressed us deeply inside. As we remembered our early thoughts when we had seen the boy treated with favor, we felt uncomfortable. I did not feel any resentment to him for what he had caused to me that night either. I was truly sorry for that young boy and his life which had brought him such a sad end. Probably Muller did not need him or was not satisfied with him anymore. Another possibility may be that the boy had seen something he was not supposed to. Whatever the reason, which we could only try to guess, the boy was now lying under the ground, buried like a dog in an anonymous, disrespected grave. Anyway, it was the common procedure among the commanders to pick those prettier among the adolescent boys, who satisfied their needs. It did not save their lives, however. It only guaranteed better conditions until the inevitable. For Nazis, any Jew could stay alive until they were no longer useful.

On Sundays we were usually given somewhat better and more caloric food. In the mornings, Germans and Capos brought us to the woods for hunting. They made us stand in a circle tight to each other so that each rabbit that appeared had no way out, and they could easily shoot him dead. Later, we got rabbit soup with some meat. Surely this was not done according to our religious rules, and I knew rabbit itself was not kosher. It was a big problem for me in the beginning. I remember how I had used to feel literally sick at the very thought of eating a non-kosher meal. Here, with time, in the state of such emaciation, when we were dramatically losing weight and literally starving, we could not refuse it. These moments gave us a chance to gain some strength. We had to live; we wanted to survive.

We were definitely not used to such hard work. Digging, loading the ground, filling up wagons quickly, pushing and pulling them away - it was truly beyond our capabilities, and to make things worse, we were fed with food that contained almost no calories and could not thus give us enough strength. For many of us, it was impossible to lift a shovel up so high, and as a result, most of the ground came back down instead of inside the wagon, which drove the Nazis mad. "I will show you how to work!" they screamed in such moments. Sometimes they hit us; sometimes they showed us how to do it right. Once, two of them were satisfied that they had managed to completely fill in one wagon quicker than us. How cruel and contemptuous! They did not have to work all the time in that way, they ate regular food until they were full, and were so proud to feel better than we were. What they were truly best at was convincing us that we were good for nothing.

Obviously, we were not allowed any breaks during the shifts. However, we tried somehow to make up for it; there was always one of us watching carefully, and whenever our supervisors disappeared, we used to grant each other a short moment of rest. What a relief! To stretch our backs and breathe calmly for a moment! Once, however, such an illegal break finished quite badly for me. I did not realize I was being watched and let myself rest a moment. I was brought back to reality with a metal bar battering me fiercely and repeatedly on my back and face. I felt blood running down my mouth and I realized my few teeth had just been broken. I felt so miserable. Was this punishment, accompanied by swearwords addressed at me, really appropriate to my offence? I was punished with a brutal beating for just relieving my exhausted body. I recalled the pain I had gone through for trying to alleviate my hunger. Now I felt similar soreness overwhelming my body and soul. However, I could not let myself breakdown. I immediately got back to work, swallowing my humiliation and regret along with my warm blood.

Weeks passed by and nothing changed, except for our weight going persistently down. We tried to keep up with the time, but we were never certain if our count was correct. We had no access to the everyday world outside. Each day was the same and we lived in constant fear of what could happen next and what could have already happened to our closest families. In such conditions, the perception of time changes completely. An hour felt like a year; a day of hard work with meager food and lack of water seemed a century. During exhausting hours of arduous overworking, we all prayed for water, but it always used to remain our dream, unless the sky came with help and poured down some rain on our exhausted, parched bodies.

One day, we were ordered to write letters to our families, giving them our address so that they could contact us back. What a privilege! We could not believe it! I was so happy to be given such an opportunity. I wanted to contact both my parents in Wodzislaw and my dear brother in Zarnowiec, to enquire after them all, find out how they felt and if they had enough food to eat, ask how things were, and of course, let them know I was safe and sound, and they didn't have to worry about me. Unfortunately, I could not recall precisely the address in Wodzislaw. Since, however, not long ago I had to remember exactly the location of my uncle in Zarnowiec, I knew how to reach my brother. As a result, I could write only to him, but still, I was happy about that unexpected possibility.

"Dear brother, I miss you." I wrote. "I am concerned about you. What has happened to you since we separated? Please write to me." It was just a short note I sent, giving him my address to write back. We were given small postcards, which obviously could not hold much text. It was clear we could not write what we wanted. Everything was done under strict supervision. Nazis must have read carefully what we wrote there. Anyway, the main thing was to get any sign from my dear Jacob, proof he was still alive. I waited impatiently and apprehensively, but to my great relief and happiness, soon I got a parcel! Inside, there was a short letter, too. My dear brother informed me that he was worrying about me: "I hope you are all right. I have been so concerned about you. What conditions do you have there?" He sent me some food; he was so kind. After such a long time, thanks to Jacob, I tasted chocolate and was able to remember again the taste of real bread. I was truly touched. He must have been starving himself. He still had unknown future ahead of him, and as meager as they were, I had regular rations here. I wrote him back informing him I was doing all right: "It was so kind of you and thank you for your care, but you shouldn't have sent me food. You need it more than me." I wanted also to convince him I was well and safe, which would give him some encouragement and comfort. Soon I got another reply. My brother was about to change his location: "There are letters all around the town encouraging us to go out from hiding. We are promised good work and food in Radom."

It was the last time I heard from him. I never had a chance to find out what Radom was like for my dear brother. He never reached that place; he never was meant to. Only after years, just like other survivors, did I learn of how what we took for an opportunity to contact our families was a cruel trap. It was again a carefully planned action aimed at those of us Jews who could possibly be staying somewhere free, safe and sound. First of all, we provided our tormentors with the addresses of our relatives, many of whom were hiding. Then, by sending our short letters, we reassured them that labor camps did exist, that Germans did keep their word and that it was useless to stay in hiding when people could be provided with regular work and food. Many poor creatures around all Poland fell into this death trap. Many did not have any more strength to live in fear; many were lured by the promise of food. Both my brother, Jacob Hirsh, and my uncle, Abraham Lenczner, succumbed to those promises of shelter. Together with all others, they were loaded onto trucks and trains, which remorselessly took them to their last destination; Treblinka or Auschwitz. I myself cannot be certain to which of these concentration camps my dear brother and uncle were taken. The fact is that anywhere they went, the outcome was the same. They were cruelly deceived and brutally murdered for no reason.

Of course I could not know it all at that time; I was growing apprehensive and hopeless when he stopped responding. I imagined all possible variants of events, but the truth hit me only after the war, when I was trying to put the pieces of my crashed world back again. At that time, we still did not suspect the worst our tormentors were planning; it was difficult, but we still had not given up. Who could see in their mind's eyes such grotesque and unimaginable horrors that Nazi Germany had planned so carefully and scrupulously for us, the Jewish nation?

In the meantime, months passed, each day filled with hard work, curses and hits from our torturers. We were not certain of our future, we had no news from home, we had not a clue what was happening in the world we left a long time ago. We were getting thinner and weaker, but at the same time, the desire to survive was deep inside giving us strength.

Poor, filthy living conditions and lack of proper hygiene contributed to the spread of lice and this with time brought about typhus typhoid. Our camp was not an exception for this; inmates and Nazis were affected alike. The suffering we went through seems beyond any words. We were extremely weak and dizzy, with high fever, sweating, and vomiting. The intensifying diarrhea, which accompanied the typhoid fevers, was depriving us of the rests of strength. A few steps walking seemed at that time a tremendous effort. They relocated us to the cabins with bunk beds; I myself lay on the upper part. I shook all over, trying not to faint because of the high temperature I had. Every time I tried to lift my head, I went weak and dizzy, my eyes became dim, and I couldn't see a thing. However, severe waves of both nausea and diarrhea were genuinely remorseless, making me, every now and then, pull myself together and get up for the bathroom. I helped myself by holding tight to the wall and bed so that I would not fall down. Then almost on all fours I was tried to reach the toilet, from where I couldn't go out, since I was so exhausted after the diarrhea attack. After, yet even weaker, I virtually crawled back to my bed again, making a superhuman effort to climb up from where after a moment I had to rush again, over and over again. It seemed an endless torture.

The typhoid epidemic took its toll; it took approximately 80 percent of the camp. My body was malnourished and emaciated; I felt weaker by the day. Yet, against all odds, I was one of those few who managed to survive. Since among the victims there were many Nazis too, we were relocated to Plaszow Gulag II, outside Krakow, the camp depicted in the movie Schindler's List[1].

This camp is the place I now reach with my family, almost sixty years later. I could not show them Gulag I, as it had been destroyed. Instead, we see the houses of the commandants, Muller and Gett, still standing intact. Now, however, they are occupied by local families. Do they know the history of this place? Do all of them know what these walls that shelter them now used to be? Do they know what happened here? Does it matter for them at all?

The entrance to the camp was from Jerozolimska Street. The Nazi tactic was incomprehensible; they used for its location two Jewish cemeteries, built as early as 1887. Thousands of gravestones were destroyed, thousands of souls devastated, desecrated, neglected. When I arrived there, in August of 1943, the first thing I saw was women working hard carrying heavy gravestones. Under German supervision and observed carefully from

---

1   Schindler's List, directed by Stephen Spielberg and written by Steven Zaillian; a 1993 biographical film based on the novel Schindler's Ark by Thomas Keneally of the true story of Oskar Schindler, a German businessman, member of Nazi party and owner of the factory, where he employed Jews. Bribing Nazi officers, he saved around 1,100 Polish Jews from death

watchtowers located all around, they were building an asphalt road using Jewish tombstones; the road was to be built on the bodies of Krakow Jews, buried here long years before. What a grotesque scenario! Jews forced to build themselves a place of their own humiliation and deprivation on their holy place. For us, Jews cemeteries are to remain untouched until the end of the world; now we Jews, were forced to destroy it ourselves. My heart ached thinking what perverse and cruel methods the Nazi had chosen. Maybe it was truly the end of the world?

Since the work was obviously beyond their capabilities, the women kept dropping the tombstones all the time, which in turn made them cry, but they did not give up. I stood with others watching them over the electric wire fencing. It was a truly depressing view: shaved heads, sunken cheekbones, grey faces with hollow eyes, thin and hopeless. Forced to overwork, exploited, and humiliated. Their image will stay with me forever. They did not resemble women at all. I cried inside, realizing we all looked like that. We were no longer humans. According to Nazi classification, we actually never had been humans. Due to the hunger we were exposed to, lack of proper care and all other atrocities we experienced, our bodies truly lost their human countenance. Once we had been strong, handsome people. Now we looked like hopeless skeletons covered with skin, yet still moving, infested with lice, wearing filthy uniforms. Disease, degradation, and death were everywhere. I made friends only to see them vanish, murdered or not able to endure the terror. Nazis were working hard to deprive us of all humanity, strength, and hope.

I was assigned to working in building construction; the company's name was KRUP. We were to construct new buildings. The first house that was to be build was quite high; it had a few floors. We climbed up the wooden planks, pushing heavy wheelbarrows filled with concrete upstairs. They must have been heavier than our skinny bodies. We passed one another bricks, throwing them from upstairs to those standing further down. We were rushed all the time to both catch and throw the material. No wonder tired and weak people often missed and hit with heavy bricks on their heads. No German ever paid attention to it, when bricks cut our heads open. Nor could they have cared less when we were weighted down with wheelbarrows. It was their goal to exhaust us with emaciating work beyond our strengths; if the process could be helped along with risky jobs, it was even better for them.

It was here that I had witnessed the selection of Jon. Here I had walked scared stiff to the hill, to experience the death sentence by shooting. Here I had experienced one of the most meaningful *Yom Kippur* of my life, when unknown hands had pushed me inside the pit and sheltered me from all the bullets fired at my weak body.

We walk here now with my family watching the remains of the tombstones left after Schindler's List had been shot. There is a fragment of the original fence, now obviously with no electricity running inside, but most of the ground is covered with grass. What the Nazi did not manage to obliterate themselves is slowly disappearing with time.

I manage to find the place of the execution. It is not marked at all either. I know what this ground hides. I myself was there for a while. Had fate decided differently, had it decided a different role for me, I would be lying here inside, under this grass too, among other dry bones of anonymous lives, of emaciated prisoners who became nothing but numbers. This massive grave is no exception in Poland. There are plenty more, not only in concentration camps. Most of the towns and cities with Jewish communities witnessed massive executions in different places, which time covered with grass, trees, and buildings - but first of all, with forgetting. My thoughts return again to my parents and siblings. Are they also buried somewhere carelessly? Do others tread on them without even knowing it? It will forever disturb me to know they have no proper place of eternal rest.

At the exit to the camp, we meet a man who, as it turns out, initiated building a museum of Plaszow, Mr. Kozlowski. He is fascinated with my story. Interestingly enough, I happen to be the first and the only survivor alive who came back and could bear witness with my testimony. My story of suffering and horror is, at the same time, a historic document, and they lack these here. On the other hand, I am obviously looking for pictures and any documents from the time of the camp's existence, and I hope he can help me too. We promise each other to stay in touch and send each other what we are looking for.

Four

It is a very emotional day for me, and I become a little relieved to finish it visiting neutral places. We go to the Old Town and Market Square. As a child, I heard about the beauty of Krakow but obviously had never been here. Now, I am walking through its streets with my wife and four children. Who would think, sixty years ago, that fate would turn this way for me? We write down our names in Schindler's book, as survivors. I never met him, though he was so close with his factory during the war. I am watching my children touched to tears, listening to the story of the pharmacy in the Krakow ghetto[1], whose owner also saved the lives of many Jews. In my heart I thank God I have lived until these days, that I have lived until such time when I can talk about my suffering to my family, somewhat releasing the burden I am convicted to carry this lifetime, and they are supportive and understanding. I thank God life is better for them and they are spared the tragedies I went through. I thank God the only way they can experience such fate is through the history, through what they can hear and read, and through the remains of what apparently belongs now to the past.

I am in Krakow again, long years after the liberation, a free man with his wife and children. I enter and leave Plaszow camp again, this time of my own decision. I can also decide what to do next. That was not the case in 1944.

---

1   The only working pharmacy enclosed within the Krakow ghetto, which belonged to Tadeusz Pankiewicz, a Polish pharmacist permitted to continue his work; Pankiewicz was awarded Righteous Among the Nations title by Yad Vashem; published a book called The Krakow Ghetto Pharmacy

FIVE

In January 1944 we again changed our location. They decided to move us from Plaszow to the labor camp in Pionki, near Radom. There was an ammunition factory there.

Working in an ammunition factory would seem better and easier than toiling in building construction. However, we had to work very hard at the factory as well. What was different this time, however, was that we worked together with people from the village, who came to work in the morning and after the workday were allowed to go back home. On the one hand, it was a great relief for us prisoners to see civilian people living their free lives, to have a proof that outside there was still, more or less, with regular life going on. On the other hand, their presence reminded us that we were not a part of that life, though we could not find any good reason for that. We asked ourselves what difference there was between us and those people? What wrong we had done to be punished so severely, to be deprived of everyday normal life, of our families and regular safety; to be sentenced to slave work in the cold winter and in the heat of the summer; to be exposed to hunger, suffering, humiliation, constant fear, and uncertainty about when and how our lives would be over?

We had reached such a level of both starvation and humiliation that we waited for the workers to finish eating in the canteen so that we could rush and pick over any leftovers from the plates and to lick them until no speck was left. We were vigilant all the time, careful not to miss the moment when we were finally able to run impatiently to the canteen and look for any food remains.

The ravaging hunger made us look for all possibilities of filling our stomachs, at least only to alleviate the burning inside a little. During summer months they needed some people to work in the fields. Luckily, I was in such a group, and we were responsible for growing carrots. We picked up one every now and then, looked carefully around, and rubbed the mud into our trousers and ate it. These carrots seemed tastier and sweeter than any carrots we had ever eaten before or we would eat after; such was our hunger. We prayed that this job, which had saved us in a way, would last forever. Thanks to working in the fields, we were not so hungry or weak; but unfortunately, after a certain period of time, we had to go back to the ammunition factory.

Then, the factory itself came with help for us. There, they produced gunpowder for bullets and the main component of this was alcohol, constituting up to 70 percent of the whole material. It was stored in flat cans, a half-liter each. Because the shape made it quite easy to hide them under our clothes, we tried every now and then to smuggle some cans, which we offered in exchange for food. The workers eagerly cooperated with us, as they liked to relax themselves by drinking alcohol, especially in those hard times. Germans, however, controlled everything, including how much and what product people were allowed to buy, and alcohol was not easy to obtain. In return for percentage beverages, the workers gave us sandwiches, bread and cheese, which they brought from their homes. It was such a relief to our starving bodies.

We were fully aware of the risk we took, and we realized we could face, at the very least, severe corporal punishment, if the Nazis caught us. Even I myself, who had already experienced the consequences of sneaking food, could not contain my overwhelming hunger, which was stronger than my fear or common sense. We had reached the level of starvation where the physical body's needs take over any rational or spiritual values, where men find themselves unable to function properly, to think of anything else other than finding the way to satiate the persistent call from the stomach. Under such circumstances, no mind is able to ask questions about safety or morality. We knew the food we ate was not kosher, but should we resign and die of starvation?

The procedure of alcohol and food exchange continued with success until one day when one of us was caught with an alcohol can in the narrow passage we went through each day. Nazis took the can from him and beat him all over. We were all frozen; it could have been any of us! Scared about how it would end, we stood by silently observing. However, they soon let him go, and we all were relieved it was over.

The following Sunday morning, we were lined in threes and taken to a huge plot, where as usual the Nazis made us practice putting our hats on and taking them off in unison according to their orders. When we were coming back, we passed the gallows, and suddenly, to our astonishment, one of our fellows was caught and dragged there. We realized it was the one who was caught smuggling alcohol. Our assumption that he had escaped serious punishment proved naïve. The Capos knew what to do. The scared victim managed to ask them, "What are you doing? You are Jews, just like me!" We all were deeply saddened by their answer, "Don't play with us. Let us have your head and shut up!" They hanged him apparently with no hesitation or doubt. All of us had to watch. We all were shocked and depressed. Obviously, each of us understood the message too. Despite our hunger, most of us quit the business; our lives were more precious.

Time passed slowly and soon we welcomed the summer of 1944. How could the sun shine and such beautiful days come despite this continuing horror? It had already been five years since that brutal invasion, which deprived us forever from calm and carefree hearts. We continued our hard work and performed obediently all the orders. *Mutze auf, mutze ab!*[1], short nights, long days, starvation, and fear. We slowly decreased in number; more and more of us were giving in to inhumane conditions and passing away. I was still there, despite all cruelties aimed at depriving us of any life energy.

Soon a new decision arrived; we were to be transferred from Pionki to Auschwitz. This again brought apprehension to our hearts. Though we could never be certain we would be alive the next hour, a bigger change always made us deeply nervous and insecure. We had no idea why they were taking us there. We were not familiar with the name. We could suspect a little, of course, and put some things we heard together, but we could never be certain what our torturers were planning for us. We were very weak and not efficient as we used to be. Maybe they did not need us anymore. Dreadful thoughts and premonitions were born in our minds and did not let us breathe calmly.

Things did not bode well, anyway. The train arrived pulling wooden cattle-

1   *Mutze auf, mutze ab*, German, "hats off, hats on," usual order by Nazis in concentration camps

trucks. My heart contorted, and I felt I was going to be sick at the sight of it, having in mind my last trip from Miechow. Again, however, I was crammed inside among hundreds of other poor bodies. We were not humans for them, so why should they treat us better than animals then? It was true hell for us. It was mid-summer, and the sun was hot, which made the journey much more difficult to endure. Everyone was gasping for air; the heat was unbearable; a tiny barred window barely let any oxygen in. The resulting stench was horrible. People were cried, fainted, lost their senses. We all would have done anything for a small sip of water. We were extremely parched. It is no wonder that many of us did not endure the conditions during the long journey. We were already very weak, and as a result, people died all the time. It was also a part of the Nazi plan; they meticulously arranged each opportunity so they could get rid of more Jews.

There was no space to put the dead bodies; we didn't know what to do with them. Finally, we had no other choice but to simply load them on a pile and sit on them so that other people would have some room to stand. In such a way, we continued our tremendous journey to the unknown, dead and alive together.

How much all these events constantly shaped us! In my mind I went back to the late summer of 1939 in Szczekociny when I first saw dead bodies. That moment came as the beginning of the end to my safe world where death was always shocking and sad. After all we had seen so far, we were slowly becoming numb and indifferent. Death was omnipresent, surrounding us ceaselessly and lurking sinisterly. We could not be sure we would be alive the next minute. We somehow had already died inside together with our families, our gone worlds and what we came to experience instead. Unfortunately, I had not yet seen the worst of the death I was to see during this cruel war.

The train slowly took us to our next destination with a growing toll of our dead companions. More and more people lost consciousness; more and more broke down. I found the conditions severe as well, but I somehow managed to keep myself quite stable. My mind was focused on the name: Auschwitz. I was filled with a growing premonition. About halfway the train suddenly stopped for a while at some station. Another train came from the opposite direction, also loaded with people who no longer resembled human beings – skinny, grey, and dispirited. It was a good occasion to get some information from them! We started to ask questions through the barred windows. We spoke Yiddish. It turned out they were coming from Auschwitz. It couldn't be that bad then, if people were coming back from there as well, we thought in the beginning. Our hopes were quickly dashed with further information we heard. Although they did not know where they were being transferred, they thanked God they had come out alive. Any place seemed better than Auschwitz, according to what they were saying. The picture they revealed to us slowly sent shivers down our spines, depriving us of any remains of the strength we might have had. It seemed we were going directly to hell on earth, right into Death's arms.

"Forget the idea that you will get out of there," they said. "There is only one way out – with the flames through the chimneys! Crematoria are working day and night, burning all the Jewish bodies into ash!"

We couldn't believe it. It seemed a dreadful nightmare. We could imagine everything, and we thought nothing would surprise us more than what we had seen so far, but crematoria burning people? It seemed incomprehensible.

This piece of news made us all scared and depressed. So, we were going to end up in flames. Most people had completely broke down, but it is true what they say, Hope dies last. So, we comforted ourselves. If we have survived all the turbulent moments until now, we thought; if these people managed to get out of there a different way than through a chimney, maybe there would be a chance for us too?

However, I decided not to remain a sheep led to slaughter. This was the moment I made my decision. Since there was a great threat I would not survive anyway, I felt it had become worth the risk to try to escape from the train. In the worst case, I would die more quickly, I thought.

"I am not going any further," I said to the rest of the people. They looked at me not understanding what I was talking about. "I am going to escape through the window." Naturally, this statement brought about confusion and ferment. A chaos of disagreement and havoc resulted. "They will shoot you right away," one man said. They tried to convince me to change my mind.

"It is too risky; you don't know what you are doing!" I heard. "I have to risk it," I replied determined. "They will not take me to a crematorium!"

"What about us? They will kill all of us! Didn't you think of it? You know their system of punishment." They looked at me carefully, obviously scared. "We all are going to be shot!" For a moment, I felt slightly discouraged. "You are putting us all in danger!" they kept reproaching me. Yes, they were right. On the roof of each truck, there was a German lying with a gun and watching us carefully. Certainly, with all the Nazi cruelty and cold rules, such action was a jeopardy not only to me, but to all who were in the truck. So what should I do now? Should I resign? I felt truly confused. I didn't want to endanger anybody's life. My comrades were dear to me. At the same time, I felt strongly that I could not stay on this train!

"If he wants to save his life, we have to help him," I heard someone say suddenly. "You're right," another voice sounded in my favor. "Listen," one of them continued, "If he has a plan, we have no right to stop him!" The situation seemed balancing a little. "Thank you," I said, looking in the direction of the supportive voices.

"They will shoot him and then come and do the same with us!" Others were not convinced. I understood both sides. "We have to help him, even in the face of the risk it entangles!" one of the men said with full conviction. He had pliers with him. Skillfully, he cut the wire in the window, which would make it possible for me to get out. Now I felt even more strongly that I should follow my inner voice. I thanked the man with the pliers and said, "I want to jump out when the train starts to move slowly. It will minimize the risk of injury. I am going to hold myself with my hands, if you, please, will lift me and hold me up." Because the window was quite small and it was high, the best solution was to go with my legs first. I could not do it myself; I needed to be lifted and supported.

The skeptics remained unconvinced, "Soon we all will be dead," they kept repeating, angry at the fact they could not control the situation. Others tried to help me climb and follow my plan. I held the window, supported by my companions, and waiting for the right moment to jump out. My heart was beating like that of a scared rabbit's in a trap, and I shook in fear. At the same time, I felt it was my chance. "If things have gone already this far, I have to try," I said to myself, trying to give myself some courage and support.

The train's wheels finally started to roll slowly. I saw the electricity poles moving faster and faster, meaning the train was speeding up. It meant the time had come; it was my moment. I turned back for a moment, just to look thankfully at the faces around for the last time - I had spent so many dreadful moments with them! I wished them the best in my heart, and there I went! I jumped out and fell to the ground alongside the train, rolling in the dirt and aching all over. I heard shots behind me. Some of the Nazis sitting on the roof must have noticed me, but luckily, none of the bullets reached me. The train continued its journey, and I hoped nobody from my truck would have to face any consequences of my decision.

I was free! After all these years in camps, secluded from the real life and the world itself, I was at large. Everything hurt after the fall, but it wasn't important. Now I had my chance. I sat a while crying, trembling and releasing all my emotions.

When I came to myself I started to look around. I felt relieved having escaped what had boded a certain death, but I was aware I was not safe yet. I had to go. But where? I had no idea where I was, I was still shocked by what had just happened and aware of the fact that the way I looked would not make it easy for me. In the close distance, I spotted a bridge with two big cement tubes. They were big enough to stand inside without crouching. A perfect shelter, I thought to myself deciding to stay there and sleep for a while. Not only did I have to gather some strength, I needed to think carefully of my next steps. It was very dangerous to stay out in public. My skinny, weak appearance, shaved head, and fearful face made me look suspicious. It could be clear that I was not only a Jew in hiding, but also an escapee from a camp. Exhausted and apprehensive, I drifted into a long-awaited sleep.

It was already dark when I woke up. I walked out of the tube feeling a growing hunger. It had been a long time since I last ate. I thought about what we were given there in Pionki. Even that watery and tasteless food from the camp seemed nourishing and worthy to me at that moment. In the distance I noticed twinkling lights from houses. Life was going on, despite the war, despite the killing process, despite the crematoria chimneys working day-and-night releasing dense smoke of stifled cries. Life was going on despite the fact that kilometers from here they were annihilating families; they were degrading people into walking skeletons with hollow, empty eyes. The world seemed to remain silent to the inequity of some of its children.

I couldn't know if the houses in front of me belonged to the Polish or Germans. I had no idea where I was and what would happen, but I thought I had no other choice but to go there. It was the direction that suggested life going on. I intended to ask where I was, and maybe I would be lucky enough to get something to eat too. I was so hungry. Fully apprehensive, I approached the first house. Outside I saw a water tap. I stopped and washed my face a little to refresh myself. I drank some too. I gathered enough courage and knocked at the door. A woman's voice asked, to my relief, in Polish, "Who is it?" "I got lost," I replied in the same language. She opened the door and looked at me. She noticed how tired I was; certainly it would take ages to recover from what I had experienced so far. She was kind enough to invite me inside to sit down. She gave me water, while I explained to her that I had gotten lost on my way and didn't know where I was. She seemed friendly, but I couldn't risk telling her all the truth. It was the war. The propaganda against Jews was well on, and who knew what could happen. Her husband brought a map and showed me the name of the place I was in. Close to this, I noticed the name of yet another village, so I told him I was supposed to get there, thanking them very much for all the help. Looking me over, he told his wife to bring me some cabbage soup. It was very kind of them. However, I dared to ask if she could bring me a sandwich instead. I was so apprehensive and fearful, I didn't want to stay any longer. She went to the kitchen and, after a while, came back, bringing a few sandwiches and a bottle of water. I thanked them truly from my heart and left the house, so content and smiling inside. I went back to my shelter, ate what I had, and prayed in my heart to thank God for His mercy. I felt so happy. For the first time, after such a long and dreadful periods, I felt calmer. When has I last eaten cheese and eggs? Or real bread? I felt it was a true feast. I didn't know what would be next, but so far I was safe and away from the dreadful camp reality with harsh life and severe voices around me all the time. I still felt very tired. No wonder I fell asleep very quickly.

I don't know how long I slept in a seemingly a dreamless sleep, but it was already a bright day when I woke up. I looked around and could not recognize the place. Where am I? What happened? After a few anxious and feverish glances around, the memory came back. It did not forget to bring also all the pain and fear, which quickly loaded me down with their weight again. I sat quietly, slowly accepting the reality, waiting for my senses to start work, and trying to think what to do next. I decided to stay where I was for some more time. This tube is definitely safer than wandering around in the unknown area, I decided.

I looked at the houses in the distance, where people were striving to lead more or less regular lives, against the brutal and dangerous reality outside. Food! My stomach was rumbling again. The night before had reminded it what pleasure and calmness a human can reach satisfying its hunger and feeling satiation. I did not want to create suspicion by going back to the same people I had visited the night before. I had said I was supposed to get somewhere else, after all. I had to stick to it. The houses in the neighborhood were fortunately located a few miles from each other, which was helpful in these circumstances. Looking carefully around, I set off with the hope to find some food again. With apprehension, I again knocked at another door not knowing what would be behind. However, Fate was on my side. Again I met a friendly family, full of compassion for me. Hollow cheeks, skinny body, fearful look - this how I was at the time. Yet they did not ask any questions. Maybe they suspected who I was? They brought me sandwiches. I looked at them with gratitude and left. Cheese again, how tasty! I walked slowly back toward my tube, satisfied things were going well and holding my treasure tightly.

Half-way there, approaching me on their horses, I saw two German soldiers. I looked around but had nowhere to hide. It was too late anyway. They had already spotted me. I could risk losing my life if they saw me fleeing and started to shoot. So it came, the end of my freedom. I am finished now, I thought, waiting to face my destiny. They reached me very quickly and asked some questions in German. I decided to pretend I couldn't understand them. German is very similar to Yiddish. I could have right away betrayed my true nature. Instead, I gave them some irrelevant answers in Polish. My heart was again contorting with fear. I felt I was facing imminent death, but I was trying hard to remain stable, not to arouse any suspicion. One of the Germans left on his horse only to come back shortly in a car, while the other kept an eye on me. "Get inside!" they ordered right away.

So, my freedom is over I thought, with a broken heart. I had a few nice moments before the inevitable. I was really scared and at the same time could not show it. They could have killed me on the spot and I knew it. They could have told me to take my trousers off to see I was circumcised, which would be a proof I was Jewish. None of these things happened. Maybe nothing seemed that wrong? I sat silently trying to calm the millions of thoughts running through my head. Finally, the car stopped. We had reached the place. The time to meet my death, I thought. They led me to a building that turned out to be a prison. Inside, I met some Polish who were incarcerated for political reasons. I didn't know if it was good or bad I was there. All that mattered was that I was still alive. Uncertain of the future and troubled by the sudden course of events, I tried to fall asleep. I decided to avoid any talks with the prisoners; I thought if I didn't speak, they wouldn't realize I was Jewish. In the early morning, we were gathered quickly and marched to a nearby camp. After a short while, we arrived. It was Auschwitz.

So here I was. I had risked my life, miraculously managed to escape from a death train, lived happily for a few hours and ended up at this place anyway. It seemed all roads led to Auschwitz for Jews. Did every road also lead to its chimneys? One cannot escape their fate, and I am to join my travel companions now, I thought. Yet, I couldn't know at that time, that I was luckier than they were. I had managed to escape a big selection on the ramp right after the train arrival, which was a regular camp procedure once the wagons crammed with poor victims arrived. I had been fortunate enough to miss seeing the Nazis drag the bodies of my dead travel companions onto the ramp like they were worthless bags. I had missed the cruel, hateful orders accompanied by numerous blows. I missed the meeting with the almighty selector, Dr. Mengele. He was known as the Angel of Death, yet, he acted a god here, in his own yard. His thumb expertly moved right and left. These two directions were said to represent life and death, according to what the doctor saw and decided. The lucky ones who met his expectations were saved for work. Some did not fulfill the requirements; they were too thin and too weak. What would be the use of them? These went right to gas chambers, thinking they were going to take a shower. All this I was told and found out myself with time, just like the truth that, in fact, both directions were sentences of death. It was only the question of time. Die now, or after the emaciating and devastating work.

In the meantime, I stood obediently in the queue with other inmates for registration. I could not have believed what that meant until I saw it myself. Tattooing. They tattooed us with numbers. It was our registration for entry to the camp. Under cold orders I gave them my left forearm, like all the others before me. German precision and experience made it last only a few moments; for me, an Orthodox Jew, it was the eternity of suffering and humiliation. In my head I heard God's words from our *Torah*, "You shall not make gashes in your flesh for the dead, or incise any marks on yourselves: I am the Lord."[1] My soul was crying. All the degradation I had experienced reached its utmost in that moment for me. I was no longer Izyk Mendel Borensztajn, no longer a human. My new name was B-94. I had become a number. A peculiar baptism let me into this new world. Only now could I join the group of Gypsies, with whom I would work and live from now on, as B-94.

---

1   Quotation from Leviticus 19:28

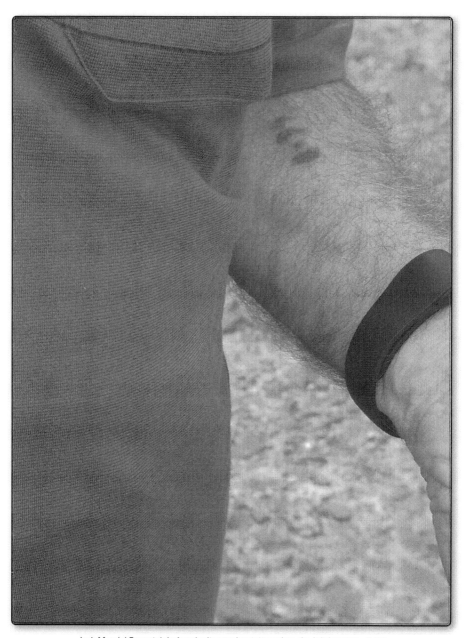

Izyk Mendel Bornstein's Auschwitz number tattooed on the left forearm - B-94

SIX

I am looking at my left forearm and the number that has remained with me through all these years not letting me forget for a single moment from where I have come. It is August 3, 2004, and the second day of my stay in Poland comes to an end. The most meaningful event of this trip is still about to come; tomorrow I will visit Auschwitz. How will I react? It wasn't that difficult in Plaszow, since the construction of the camp was to a certain extent destroyed. The main proofs for what it used to be are the gloomy watchtowers and the barbed wire. I know, however, that in Auschwitz the main shape of the camp was preserved, and a museum was created there. I will enter apparently the same site. How will I react?

Old images come back to me: crematoria; gas chambers; constant fear and starvation; yelling of Nazis; shots from their guns; barking of their dogs; new trains coming over and over again, unloading their innocent cargo right into the greedy mouths of the merciless Nazi ovens. No matter how many years pass, these images remain forever vivid in my mind, as if it all happened only yesterday. I am moving in time, learning to live again and to function with my memories engraved in my mind and heart, but the emotions accompanying this period of my life will for always retain the same strength.

I can't sleep. I keep tossing and turning, but I do not change my mind about going back again. At the same time, my younger son, Zvi, who carries the name after my dear younger brother, has a life-changing experience, of which I am told only later. In the middle of the night, he starts to scream hysterically, waking up his elder brother, Yossi, who shares the room with him, right next to ours. However, although I can't sleep much either, I don't hear that noise. It does wake up my wife, though, who rushes to the window, thinking there is some drunkard or even a fight going on. Not seeing anything, she comes back to bed a little confused.

In the other room, Yossi is trying to handle the situation. "Zvika, what happened? Did you have a nightmare?" he asks him carefully. "It is not a dream! It is very vivid. I am still there!," Zvika says, "I am standing with a crowd of men next to the door to some building. All of us are naked. There is a short, very old man in front of me, and there are two Nazi guards standing on both our sides. They can't open the door from the inside because of us crowding there." His voice becomes more dramatic now, yet he continues. "They are trying to push us away, to open the door and let us inside. One of the Nazis takes his gun and hits the old man standing in front of me, right into his head! He is bleeding! Now I understand, they want to kill us all there, inside!"

The situation stuns Yossi a little, but he acts quickly. Without hesitating, he immediately gives Zvika a piece of paper and a pencil: "Draw it. Draw what you saw," he says. Still shocked, Zvika is trying to picture what he had just experienced.

The next morning we set off to Auschwitz.

Symbolically, we start with Birkenau where I was brought that summer of 1944. From meters ahead, I can see its gloomy shape and feel I am shivering and shrinking with pain inside. It looks horrifyingly the same - the gate, the tower, the railway, the barracks. Inside, some of the buildings have been destroyed, but indeed, the general view and outline is the same. We enter the tower and watch the enormous land. Its view is really depressing, even without experiencing the time when the camp was operating at full scale. I look at these buildings but cannot be sure which one I used to live in. They all look the same. In my mind, I see the shadows of inmates, intimidated and emaciated skeletons, all alike, with no hair, and all dressed in striped, filthy outfits. I see the smoke coming out of the crematoria chimneys; I see Nazis in their watchtowers all over the land, carefully following each one of our steps with their cold eyes and ready to shoot for the slightest disobedience. I feel this atmosphere of fear and terror very strong and clearly, as if I were still there, during the dark age of the Holocaust.

Suddenly I am brought back to the present with the noises behind. It turns out our arrival at the camp has coincided with the visit of a group of Israeli students from Reut school in Jerusalem who are visiting concentration camps in Poland. Surprisingly enough, it is the group Gienia was talking about at Wysoka Synagogue. Among them, I see Gienia herself. It seems an unbelievable coincidence.

Gienia points at me and says, "I am not a survivor of this camp, but he is." They all feel honored meeting me, and consider it divine intervention. I am not surprised they want to listen about the camp from me and hear my personal story. It is not easy and requires a lot of strength from me, but I know I want to face it until the end, to release some of its weight, and of course, to let those young people hear the camp story from an authentic source. I come back again to those dark, gloomy days of my imprisonment and tell them what I remember...

Birkenau used to be a small village before. Nazis turned it into a sub-camp of Auschwitz, together with nearby Monowitz. The main complex was located around three kilometers away. We lived in overcrowded, stable barracks. Inside, there were two rows of three-level bunk beds. Actually, "bed" was not the right name for these -simple wooden boards hammered together. One lousy, thin, filthy blanket was meant to suffice for five people lying next to each other, and sometimes even virtually on top of one another, due to lack of space. We slept on bare boards. Some had paper sacks, some did not have anything to cover themselves with. Still, although it is difficult to believe, these places to sleep were better than in Plaszow, where we slept almost on the floor. There were hundreds of prisoners in one building, even if there were other buildings standing empty. The only light source was tiny skylights in the ceiling, which could not suffice, and as a result, inside it was gloomy and murky. Wind and rain easily got inside through the cracks. During warm days, it was incredibly stuffy, and we breathed in fact, our own breaths, circulating it over and over again, which contributed to our weakness.

There was no real toilet. We had a concrete structure built above the ground in a separate room, with a long row of holes. There was no pit below the latrines. They were not deep either. Once full, we had to clean them out ourselves. Obviously, we did not have such a luxury as toilet paper, and we were not allowed to use the toilets when we needed to either. There was a special, limited time specified by the Capo when all of us together were allowed to relieve ourselves, whether we actually needed it at that particular time or not. We had to somehow overcome the shame and natural inhibition, which was the biggest barrier.

Nothing was humane here, and Nazis reminded us all the time that we were not humans. Each action, each step, all conditions were carefully planned to strip us slowly and painfully of any self-esteem. Everything they did served one: degradation, dehumanization, humiliation. We were treated as animals, nothing more. In the camp, we found we were limited to the numbers that had been tattooed on our arms during registration. We were shaven completely, all our bodies; we had to give away anything we brought with us including shoes and clothes. I myself, coming already from previous camps, did not have anything anyway.

According to Nazi philosophy, we did not need hair on our heads; we did not need clothes other than striped tatters; we did not need shoes other than wooden, uncomfortable clogs. Too big? Too small? Two right or two left? It was our problem. No one had the courage to complain. Who would risk having their shoes taken away or suffering the punishment for daring to speak? Instead, we tried to organize and exchange things among each other. Altogether, comparing with Plaszow, Auschwitz was a place of much more severe conditions. There, one could see the resemblance to the labor camp. Here, with crematoria and gas chambers working day and night, we had no doubts that we were in a factory of death. It was obvious there was only one future for us. The only question was: when.

With time we became aware of more and more facts of this cold, meticulously planned scenario, in which we were playing major roles. Our former clothes and property went to Germany. The families of our torturers were wearing our clothes. In the opinion of Nazis, what they gave us to wear was more than enough. We did not deserve anything but humiliation and death. In such conditions, it was impossible to remain without lice. We couldn't even wash ourselves carefully; the rags we wore did not help either. Later we found out our hair also found its use, as they used it to produce felt, and they filled mattresses with it. Nothing could escape German meticulousness.

When I came to Auschwitz, there were two crematoria working, out of five that had been active before my arrival. They did not stop working. Transports arrived all the time, bringing the enemies of Nazis that they had to get rid of. During this war, we understood clearly that even women, children, and babies could be enemies of the Third Reich. The new order rulers had to act immediately, annihilating all Jews, no matter their position or age. The resulting smoke odor coming from the chimneys burning their bodies was unbearable. The smell of burnt flesh penetrated our lungs, going deep inside. It is impossible to forget it.

We worked in such conditions day by day, week by week, month by month, and we learned to accept our fate. Most of the time we worked building cannons. It was hard work and the food we got was definitely did not cover our needs. My weight was constantly going down, but I was determined to survive against all odds. Deep inside us, a persistent belief was striving: one day the war must come finally to an end, and we would tell everybody what we saw and what we had gone through. We often heard Nazis saying: "Even if any of you survive (but don't count on that) nobody will believe you. We will write our history of the camps for the world." This was what we dreaded and what at the same time gave us strength to fight the destiny that they were preparing for us. Our suffering and humiliation could not be in vain. Who knew, maybe there were even some our relatives waiting for us? Maybe somewhere, somehow, some of them also managed to survive, and now, like us were waiting for liberation so that we could be united again?

The day that things changed for me started as usual. We got up at early dawn, we received our rations, we drank our everyday black liquid they called "coffee" and in sips with our slices of dark stones they called "bread." Was I getting mad from hunger, or were these rations actually growing smaller every day? We set off for work and proceeded according to the orders. Suddenly, in the middle of the work, I felt a great pain piercing my stomach and groin. I could neither move, nor could I control it. I sat down on the ground, waiting for it to pass. Next came a series of events that completely changed my situation in the camp.

Immediately, I heard a yell from the side of a supervising officer: "Get up and work!" I kept moaning and holding my stomach. It must have been clear to him that I was overwhelmed with unbearable pain. It did not matter at all. He ran to me quickly and with all his power he hit me with his rifle on my back. Now I my suffering was doubled, and naturally I fell to the ground. I was not sitting anymore; I was lying, unable to move. I felt so miserable. Wasn't it enough there was something wrong inside my body? Was their hatred a punishment? If I could have, I would have continued working as usual.

The officer went away and came back with another one, carrying a stretcher. They put me onto it and took me away. I felt resigned and prepared myself to accept anything. It was too much for me. I heard my work companions saying kaddish for me. It became obvious I was not coming back; I was useless from then on. They were praying and I was going away. Is it really the end, God? Am I going to a chimney? I thought between the pain seizures. The fear was as strong as the pain. I saw them putting me into a car and driving me away. Where are we going?

We arrived at the main gate of Auschwitz, around three kilometers from where I was, and went on. I had already witnessed many disappearances of poor inmates who could no longer continue their work. Not valuable any more, they were immediately sent to gas chambers or shot. Why should it be different with me?, I thought. This is the reality of this place.

When we finally stopped, I saw a building on one side and a crematorium on the other. The door opened and they carried me out. They walked up the steps of the building, leaving the crematorium behind. Once we were inside, I could see what the building was. They had brought me to a hospital! What a relief! My death sentence had been postponed again.

The doctor came up to me and introduced himself as Karol Sperber, a Jewish prisoner. Is he going to decide whether I should stay alive or not? Is it a kind of selection process taking place here? He examined me carefully and reassured me that I should not be worried. "I am here to cure you," he said. "Now I am going to prepare you for a surgery that I will perform tomorrow. It is only a hernia," he explained. "You are not allowed to drink or eat anything before the operation. Wait calmly in your bed".

Operation. So they wanted me to stay alive? To cure me? But why? Here, in the concentration camp, where we all were sentenced to death? I could not understand it. Neither could I figure out if my condition was serious or not. Apart from the continuous pain I was feeling, I was still fearful and insecure. I didn't know how it all would finish and I grew apprehensive. The evening fell slowly, and I was carried to bed. Before we reached it, I had fainted.

I regained my consciousness the next day before the operation. They gave me local anesthesia, which did not reduce much pain. Of course they did not have proper medicines there. Why should they? Did anybody care for us or our pain? The procedure was simple; if anybody became ill or unable to work, they were killed. I still couldn't understand why I was being spared.

I don't know how long the operation was, but I woke up after in my bed in agony. Heavy bags of around five kilos had been placed on my wound. Were they deliberately adding to my suffering? I desperately tried to take them off. When Dr. Sperber came to check my condition, he found me seized with pain. I turned to him, anguished, and said, "Please, doctor, ask any of Germans to come and shoot me. I cannot stand this pain."

He looked at me and answered with certainty, "I am also Jewish, and I am here to save your life." He tried to calm me down, "Do you think I have placed these bags to hurt you? You need to be patient! The pressure from the bags makes the wounds heal faster. Please don't worry, and trust me. Two, maybe three more days, and you will be walking again."

I noticed he also had a number on his forearm. Karol Sperber was 82512. He must have come there a long time ago. My number was much smaller, but it was only due to the fact that I had arrived at the time they had started to bring in Hungarian Jews. In order to avoid assigning excessively high numbers, due to the amount of victims they already brought here, the SS authorities introduced the letters A for women and B for men, which they tattooed in front of the new number sequencing: every 20,000 new people, every 20,000 new forearms. Many years later, I found out that there were around 15,000 men with the letter B in front of our number.

"By the way," Sperber continued, "do you have any idea how much you scared me? In the middle of the operation, you started to sing Polish anthem! I was petrified that somebody would come and shoot us both!" This came as a surprise for me. I did not remember anything; I was languid and unconscious with pain but I realized what it must have meant to all who were present at the operation and around. It seemed extremely peculiar- a Polish Jew, unconscious with pain, singing the Polish anthem in the concentration camp surrounded with conquering Germans. Anyway,

I began to recover. Though still in great pain, I felt a little reassured after the doctor's visit. He treated me very well, and after all the hatred I had experienced, his kindness meant a lot.

I wondered why they had this hospital at all, since their whole plan was to annihilate our entire nation. Why did they do some treatment, like in my case, and finally, why was I saved? Only later did I realize their cruel simulation. The Nazi planned to come out of that war clean. Apparently, it was a labor camp with proper conditions: kitchens, hospital, washrooms. Nobody needed to know of the perverted use of these. Nobody could suspect what they cooked in kitchens and how little we got; nobody would guess what cruel and sick experiments they carried on in the hospital under Dr. Mengele's supervision, which I found out about later; nobody could imagine instead of having water in the washrooms, they put in Cyclone B to exterminate as many prisoners as possible at one time. It was lavished on people, while they were waiting, crammed and naked, to be washed by water. Again I heard their derisive voices: "We will tell the world our history of the camps."

I lay in bed waiting for full recovery and the pain to disappear. I tried to sleep whenever I could. All the time I thought about what happened, about my family, about the conditions I was in. Is it going to finish soon? Will I ever be able to breathe calmly and safely again? The future was a big unknown.

The day after the operation, my thinking was disturbed by the visit of a supervisor. It was Dr. Mengele, the Angel of Death. Having entered inside, in a cold and decisive voice, he ordered, "All of you out of beds to me." The patients obediently stood in the middle of the room, passing next to him right or left, according to the movement of his finger. Selection. Not everybody won the privilege to recover. Finally, he noticed me. How dare I lay in bed, disrespecting his obvious order. "Why isn't that dog coming to me?" Mengele turned to doctor Sperber, who was too scared to even look at him. He gently asked him to come to my bed, lifted the blanket, and showed him the scar.

"He is too weak; it is less than twenty-four hours after the surgery," he explained in an uncertain voice.

Mengele looked at me carefully and asked "When are you, dog, coming back to work?" I was terrified. I could not lift my eyes.

In a humble voice, looking at my blanket, I replied, "Here is my doctor standing in front of you. I will do whatever he says."

After a moment of silence, I heard Mengele say, "After this dirty dog recovers, you will teach him how to give injections and to distribute medicines and food to the patients. He will stay with you until the liquidation of the camp." He looked around and left.

Until today I don't know why he made such a decision that day. Did he like the answer I had given him? Did he have a better day? I don't think he had any mercy. A moment before he came to me, he had in cold blood sentenced a few other patients to death! With a mere movement of his thumb, this man decided: crematorium, work, crematorium, work.

The truth was that my life was saved again because of his decision. Staying with doctor Sperber meant a regular supply of somewhat better food. I could eat now until I was full, though I couldn't eat much anymore; my bowels contracted through all those years of starvation. The work was not hard, which was also important; after the hernia operation, emaciated with all those months of war, my body would not have been able to endure much more difficult work. I was working inside, and I felt useful. I was so much grateful, and thanked God in my heart for favoring me. I realized now it was a blessing in disguise; though I suffered so much, this painful experience brought me to better circumstances, where I could feel safer.

Dr. Sperber was a good teacher, and carefully explained all the rules to me. I gave shots, I gave away medicines and waited for patients to swallow them, and I also brought them food. I also supplied it illegally to prisoners outside. I was obedient and did everything as told, but I could not accept one order: we had to strictly throw away any remains of the food inside the hospital. That waste and lack of respect was both ridiculous and cruel. I knew what real hunger meant; I felt it a sin to throw away food in such times, under such conditions. Outside, people were famished. They were weakening, and had it not been for this turn of events, I would still be sharing their fate. One day, when I was looking out of the window, I was struck by a scene that would stay with me forever. I saw several poor, skinny figures in striped rags desperately eating grass. I don't care what they do with me, I will give these people food! I told myself. Each day I collected as much leftover food as possible, I opened the window and passed it to other inmates. Even the fear inside my heart could not equal the satisfaction it gave me. Never was I caught.

There is a complete silence, disturbed only with sobbing here and there, when I come to the end of my story, almost sixty years later at the camp. I see tears on most of the listeners' faces. I feel their understanding and compassion, though they are so much younger and raised in such radically different circumstances. It was difficult to continue talking at times, especially in this place, but I am satisfied I made it through and let them hear about my fate, and the camp conditions I had to endure with other inmates. I hope the students learn a proper lesson from my talking and their visit to Poland. If it happened to me and my generation, if once already such fate was created for other people, can we have any guarantee it will never happen again?

Judging by the history of the Jewish nation, unfortunately, it seems we are doomed for persecution. Even these days, those young people living in Israel cannot feel completely safe due to the situation with surrounding countries. The opinions of the contemporary Iran's president, Mahmoud Ahmadinejad, denying the Holocaust are more than petrifying. Then, having spoken to the young students, I realized it should be the moral duty of each survivor to be heard, to witness with their memories the unimaginable tragedy of millions of people and to speak for those, who were not given this privilege to talk about their suffering and humiliation. My message is very plain: Life is a gift and we need to appreciate it, never take it for granted. We do not value and respect what we consider as obvious: our health, freedom, and family life. I hope such tragedy will never happen again. I wish there were no wars or suffering in the world. We should be grateful for everything we are given and try to make our world a better place.

Before we leave Birkenau for the main camp complex, we stop at the crematorium. I look at this symbolic grave of the tragedy of our nation and can no longer hold my tears. "All my life I have been so lonely," I reveal to my children. "I have had no family." I have missed them all my life. Yes, time cured the wounds a little, but at the same time it took me further from my beloved parents and siblings; the longer I didn't see them, the more I missed them, too. I thank God my weeping was soothed by the family, I have now here with me. We pray here together, deeply touched.

Izyk Mendel Bornstein after the prayer in Auschwitz - Birkenau next to the Plaque of Remembrance at Crematorium II

I am interested in any documents of this time that may be left; therefore, we head toward the archive. I don't have any written proof for my imprisonment in Auschwitz. There, to my disappointment, a woman informs us: "It is highly improbable we will find anything; before their leaving, Germans managed to destroy 90 percent of their documents." I am saddened with this information, but we wait, nevertheless, for the results of the search. I realize how unlikely it would be to find my own certificate among all of the inmates registered here, with the mere 10 percent of the documents that survived. However, the worker comes back with a smile on her face. "I have it," she says, and we all are overwhelmed with emotion.

We had all been unable to keep track of the time in the camps, so I look with curiosity for the day I entered this valley of death and became B-94. I couldn't have known the date. It was 31st July, 1944. Today is August 4, 2004. I have come back to this horrible place exactly sixty years after I was placed here against my will. It comes as a shock.

I stand again at the gate, looking at the cynical inscription "Arbeit Macht Frei," i.e. Work Sets You Free. Nazis placed this slogan at the entrances to a number of their concentration camps, attempting to make their prisoners believe they could be free by working hard and obediently. However, no matter how hard we toiled, the only guaranteed way to become free was to die of overwork, starvation, exposure to cold, or murder at the hands of our oppressors. Never did anybody get free of this secluded, guarded, and closed area, surrounded with electric barbed wire and watchtowers with armed Nazis. Never was our freedom planned. It was their cold trick, to make us believe we could go out from there by being obedient and hardworking. In fact, work would only make us die sooner.

I enter again. Despite their meticulous plan, I have come back sixty years later. Now I am a free man, accompanied by a family I was not supposed to have. The fates decided differently. I am looking around. Not much has changed. The general shape is preserved; the buildings serve now as a museum. Only now, people walking around are here because of their own decision; they are free visitors. The wall where they used to shoot poor victims is now decorated with flags, flowers, and candles to honor the memory of the innocent, murdered souls. I still feel the gloomy atmosphere of this place; it seems the air is forever filled with our suffering and pain.

We stop at the building where Mengele used to perform his horrifying experiments on women and twins, although I couldn't know it at the time of my imprisonment here. Its windows are still sealed as they were at the time when he was performing his practices there. Everything was planned carefully; in this way nobody would see his actions or hear the women screaming; nobody could see the executions of his victims.

Inside the museum, numerous pictures are hanging; faces of victims of all ages betray fear and pain. I look at the mountain of human hair and the material woven from it, and I feel very feeble. I recall the cold process of shaving our bodies. Now I see its outcome again. The truth and the past are suddenly cast into my face with full strength. I look at the piles of shoes, brushes, suitcases, pairs of glasses, and other personal belongings stolen from innocent victims. My heart fills with pain as I look at devices of the handicapped; these poor souls were the first victims. In Nazi classification of humanity, they did not even deserve to become a number. Each of these items - each shoe, each suitcase, each toothbrush - used to have an owner; each one has their own history. I look at them and think of all the people who held them in their hands and took them along in the belief that they would come in handy here, in the "labor camp" that they had been promised. Even after all those years, even though I used to witness it, it still seems unbelievable. How can a human come up with such a plan? How can one nation create such atrocities for the other for no apparent reason? Can anyone understand?

I don't feel good, and my children notice it clearly. This visit here proves extremely draining, both emotionally and physically. Even so, I do not regret even for a single second my coming back. I already feel the importance of this visit both for me as well as for my children. Yossi suggests I go out of the camp and rest. I decide to stay. I still want to find the hospital. I look around but see only red brick buildings, whereas I remember the hospital building was white. My sons, in the meantime, walk away. As I am told later, Zvika feels a deep urge to follow his intuition, as for the dream he had the night before. After a few meters, in excitement, he suddenly starts running, to stop only at the back side of the crematorium that he had never seen before. They stand exactly at what used to be the entrance for the victims long years ago, of which they could not know, as all the information signs were placed on the other side, which was made the entrance for contemporary visitors.

"Look, Yossi," Zvika says, "this is exactly the place that was in my dream!" Before, in Birkenau, when we were praying at its crematorium, he had said with conviction, "It is not here. It is not the place." Now it proves to be precisely the same view, the same surroundings, the same entrance as he had already seen in his dream. Yossi takes a few pictures, which later we compare with the drawing made by Zvika before. We are all astonished at what we see. It is difficult to believe the drawing was not made upon the photograph.

We can't stop the question that comes so strongly to our minds: Is it a message from my dear brother, whose name we gave to my younger son? Can it be a sign from him? Does he want to show us something? Could it be he died here in Auschwitz? I am shaking. I don't know how to treat it.

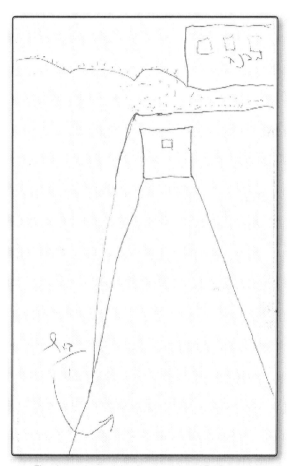

The picture drawn right after the vision of Zvi Bornstein

The place he recognized in the Auschwitz concentration camp during his first visit there

On the way back from the crematorium, my sons, still shocked after their experience, notice a white building, which draws Yossi's attention. When they come back, he asks me to follow him. "I want to show you something. Maybe this is a hospital?" We walk away, and soon I slowly fill with excitement. There, in front of me, I see the building. Yes, this is the hospital! It looks precisely the same. We walk inside, and it turns out we are lucky it is open; as an office building these days, it is locked most of the time. Another occurrence in my favor.

I go inside the building with its long corridor and numerous rooms. I remember there was a kitchen on the second floor. We check it and there it is! We try to open the doors of the rooms, but all of them are locked, to our disappointment. Only when we come back to the first floor, do I find one opened. I stand in complete astonishment, unable to say a word. Out of all the rooms that were closed, I enter the only one available. Inexplicably, it is my workroom. Here, I spent the last long weeks before we were forced to leave the camp. It is here where Dr. Sperber taught me the basics of his profession.

Izyk Mendel Bornstein in front of the window of the hospital in Auschwitz through which he gave food to prisoners

It is thanks to this place that I survived Auschwitz, as it provided me with shelter, an easier job, and, first of all, regular rations of food, which of course were not anyway to be compared with true food outside the camp, but which undoubtedly improved the condition of my emaciated body. Had it not been for the hernia case I experienced, which resulted in my arrival at hospital, I don't know how much longer I would have survived in those conditions. I recognize the window through which I used to feed other inmates toiling outside and not so fortunate to have anything to eat. I close my eyes and again see those poor beings desperately eating grass, I will never forget that terrible scene.

Amazing. Everything seems so vivid, as if it happened yesterday. I try to be calm, but each step is accompanied by strong emotions, bringing me back to those days, when this place served as our most dreadful prison, and we could not be certain we would be alive the next moment. Each step is meaningful, as it brings back terrifying memories; each takes me to the places that used to bring nothing but pain and fear.

While walking between the barracks with my family, I ask myself, How did we do it? How did we survive it? How did we manage to work all days on a few pieces of dry bread and watery liquid that they called soup? Where did we find the strength and stamina to continue, against physical and mental deprivation, against suffering and humiliation, against the death sentence hanging upon us in the air, against the solitude and broken spirits? We are standing next to the gas chambers in the crematoria. I am sobbing bitterly inside, looking at the remains of the cruel Nazi killing machine, unable to comprehend, asking myself over and over again: How can one human create such fate to the other? Sixty years ago, I was one of the numbers, one of the skinny, shaved, emaciated, and intimidated creatures trying to survive one hour more, and one more. Now I am back, a free man, accompanied by my dear, supportive family. "I am so happy I have you," I manage to tell them. "Otherwise, I would be so lonely and forsaken."

I am looking proud and touched at them. God blessed me with four children altogether, and all of them make me proud with their individual talents, all of them following the Jewish way. I have been living with my wife for over fifty years in happiness and satisfaction, welcoming new generations coming from our four children, who gave us over twenty grandchildren and a growing number of great-grandchildren. I have attended all the celebrations of Brit Mila, *Bar* and *Bat Mitzvah* [1] and weddings of the children born to my family, each time equally touched and grateful to God for bringing me to these moments, watching my family grow.

Looking back to my camp life, it was always highly uncertain I would survive the next minute, hour, or day. And yet I made it, against all odds.

---

1   *Bar, Bat Mitzvah*, Hebrew, "one to whom the commandments apply", the celebration of boys (*Bar Mitzvah*) and girls (*Bat Mitzvah*) at the age of thirteen and twelve respectively when they become responsible for their actions and bear their own responsibility for Jewish ritual law, tradition and ethics and are privileged to participate in all areas of Jewish community law

SEVEN

I met my dear wife in 1951, during the wedding of one of my best friends, Yishayahu. I was at that time a medic serving for the Israeli Defense Forces. We lived together, my three best friends and I, after we had decided to leave the *Kibbutz*. Moshe, one of them, came with a girl who drew my attention. It turned out she was only his friend, so I became brave enough to ask her to dance with me. I remember it was samba, and the girl's name was Fraidel Chedva. She came to Palestine from France in July of 1945. She was born in Strasburg, where her parents had met but her family roots were also in Poland. Her ancestors from both mother's and father's sides moved to France before the First World War from Bialystok and Dobromir. Her mother tongue was French, but she spoke also fluently German, Yiddish and Hebrew. Fate saved her too in a way, as she had managed to survive with all her family.

"We were constantly on the run," she said when she told me her story. "We were changing our location whenever risk came, permanently in fear somebody would notice us and report to the Gestapo. Most of the time we were staying in Lyon, but the day came we had to escape to Toulouse, then to Setes, to Beziers, and to Perpignan. Whenever we heard of German actions, whenever they were sending Jews to concentration camps, we set off further. We lived in not human conditions, at times had problems with finding anything to eat. I was only twelve years old when the war started, and I remember only fear from that time."

I understood her better than anybody else. Fear, starvation, escape, separation, loss of the family house - I had gone through it all and was left alone.

"There were some moments we were close to death," Fraidel continued her story. "In December of 1942, we were arrested by the Gestapo in our regular hiding place in Lyon. We survived by the miraculous intervention of the French Police and were saved by the Mercier family, who were neighbors in the same house. Two months later, in February 1943, my father, Oskar Uhri, went to help to the Jewish community and got arrested at the Jewish Welfare Organization in Lyon with eighty-six other people. Germans took his documents and left in one of the two rooms that the Jewish community occupied in the building. In the meantime, Jews were being brought from all over and packed onto a bus. My father understood that something wrong was happening and decided to escape. He went out and through the room where his documents were taken and saw it was empty. Using this opportunity he ran up the stairs to the third floor, which did not belong to Jews. He knocked at the door, but it was shut in front of him. Without too much thinking, he moved further up and then when the door was opened, he desperately put his foot preventing the non-Jew owner from closing it. It turned out the flat belonged to a governmental officer, yet he was against Germans and wanted to help my father. He agreed to come to where we lived and bring Meir and Esther, my siblings, so as to add credibility to my father who hoped to leave the building safe and unnoticed in the company of children, as a regular dweller. So it went. On the stairs they passed a German, but my father bent his head to avoid being recognized and filled with fear they all reached home safe. My father was one of three people who saved themselves that day, out of almost two hundred caught. He knew of one jumping from the toilet, and one who promised to bring back kilograms of chocolate, if released. All the others were sent to Auschwitz, as it later turned out. After that dramatic event, my parents decided to escape. Germans already had the documents of my father."

"In 1944 we were completely out of money, my parents with four children, hiding in a cellar with no windows, no sanitary facilities, each minute filled with fear we would be noticed and given to Germans. We survived only thanks to a local church in St. Symphorien Sur Coise. We were taken care of until the liberation of Lyon in September 1944."

Fraidel regretted she had no chance to master her education; during her school years, she was forced to hide on the run from the Gestapo. It was the common experience of all European Jews living in hiding. Anyway, regular schooling was not taking place during the war years; the only way to study at that time was by secret teaching in specified places under a great risk. Later, rarely did we have a chance to continue our education, we had to make our living, to take care of ourselves, find a way to build our future. Many of us were either participating within processes of rebuilding our countries, or had come to Palestine as I did to build our new shelter.

I asked Fraidel out and she agreed. We equally enjoyed each other's company and the time we spent together. During our meetings, though usually we did not meet alone but with Moshe or all the other friends, I started to realize how important she was becoming to me. Fraidel was exactly what I was looking for to start a religious family, like the one I was born into in Szczekociny. Despite the strength of my feelings and her approval, I felt I had to settle things right with Moshe. He was my best friend; I could not go against him.

"Listen," I told him, "I am thinking seriously about her. I don't want to ruin our friendship, however; if you don't agree, just say it and I am going away."

"I have nothing against it," Moshe smiled hearing that. "I told you she is just my friend. But if she agrees to be with you and marry you, I will have hair growing on my palm!"

He laughed showing his hands. Saying that, he meant how improbable this idea for him was – as likely as hair starting to grow on one's hand. He had all the rights to think like that; I was serving in the army, whereas he had become a rich man, an owner of land, and he could provide her with an easy, stable, and well-off life. Nevertheless, to my great happiness, Fraidel agreed to marry me and her parents approved of it. Sometime later, she confessed to me that her mother had told her yet even before my proposal that she would marry me.

"She had a dream," Fraidel explained to me. "A woman with a lantern was standing there saying: "It's here, it's here.'" She thinks it was your mother." I became deeply touched with this account, and I asked her to describe the woman in that dream. While she was talking, tears came to my eyes. The description suited perfectly. I had no doubt it was my mother. Could I ask for a stronger confirmation? I felt like she came and blessed my wife and my new life.

We decided to get married without thinking too much about how to overcome all the difficulties resulting from this decision. It was the year 1952, and the country was facing hard times. According to the resolution at that time, each family was allotted daily rations of food according to the number of its members. Those who could afford it tried and bought meat, dairy, and other products on the black market, paying high prices for it. However, the government was trying to prevent it as well and appointed groups of people to check civilians on buses, trains, and in their private cars to confiscate any products they would find that were treated as illegal.

I did not suffer much because of that situation. It made me think of the ghetto times, where I had to queue for a piece of bread and where we were also allowed certain amounts of food. However, compared to what I had experienced during the six war years, I felt still like I was in a paradise. We were free and living in the warm Holy Land, and the food we received sufficed us. People who were in camps with me, had died because of starvation, as Nazis systematically and cruelly reduced our portions. Nothing like that was happening here, and I was not only grateful for what I had, but also filled with hope for better days to come.

In the meantime, I was still living in the Jewish Agency apartment in Givat Rambam and Fraidel's parents were both unemployed, striving hard to make a living in a rather sloppy apartment in Petah Tikva. My monthly payment was thirty-six pounds. I saw this amount as two eighteens, which in Hebrew numerology corresponds to "life." One eighteen was for me, and the other for my wife-to-be. Words from *Avoth* [1], *Mishna*, were strong in my head: "If I am not for myself, who is there for me?" I had learned during these long, lonely years to take care of myself. I knew I had to count only on myself. Until the moment I made my three devoted friends in *Kibbutz*, I was completely alone, striving to build my life from the beginning; I was in the new country, I didn't know anybody, and I was dragging with me the memories of six years of oppression. I was yearning for my family, but slowly had to learn the cold truth that I had been left alone. These six years had destroyed my outer and inner world forever. I had survived, I was learning everything again, but I realized that after what I had gone through, there was no return to the beginning. Inside, I would carry my wounds and suffering forever, together with the inconsolable cry for my beloved family.

Yet, at the same time, this situation had taught me independence and strength. Nothing could be difficult for me anymore when compared to

1   *Avoth*, Hebrew, "fathers", "patriarchs", a tractate of *Mishna* composed of ethical maxims of Rabbis

what I had left behind in Poland. Now, when I had to organize the wedding reception with no family of my own and my wife's unemployed parents, the fates came with help. People around me supported me in numerous ways. Within the previous years of my hard work in the tile factory and later with concrete production, I had managed to save six hundred pounds, which was at that time quite a lot of money and made me feel like a rich man. My friends, who shared the apartment with me, one by one settled down, and left it, which enabled me to act according to my own plan. I immediately hired a worker to build a kitchen with a roof around the two existing rooms. I couldn't give him more than ten days to complete the works if I wanted to make it ready on time. Right in the middle of the preparations, I found a notice on the wall left by the city council officers ordering me to immediately stop any building construction. I put the notice into my pocket and asked the worker to hurry up, promising him some extra sum of money in return.

In the meantime, I was trying hard to organize the reception. Due to the difficult market situation, the banquet hall owner informed me that he had trouble finding enough food for the two-hundred-fifty guests that Freidel's father invited. The doctors I worked with were the only ones I could share my problem with.

"Mendel," said one of them, "Since I am the owner of a fishpond in Mikhmoret, I will give you with pleasure more than two-hundred-fifty carps as your wedding present. However, I don't know how to help you with their delivery."

He seemed a little worried with that, but the other doctor, Dr. Doitch interrupted him with a smile, "I will sign a driving slip for you allowing you to go by an ambulance, apparently to bring a patient." It seemed a very challenging and to a certain extent crazy idea, but I did not have any other solution. Dr. Doitch wanted to help me, as he truly liked me. Actually, I wasn't much afraid, as all the Military Police Officers knew me well. Each time they stopped me to check my license, they used to salute me and wish me a good journey.

I was also helped with organizing drinks, and when I brought it all to the banquet hall, the manager was truly happy and couldn't stop thanking me.

And I was happy to see later that all the guests were satisfied and content with the reception. I still can see Chuber Rabbi dancing with my wife and holding two ends of a white handkerchief, and everybody around clapping their hands.

Yet, my happiness would forever carry with it a portion of grief and sorrow. Mother, father, I thought, Why can't you be here with me to bless me and see my joy? How much I would have given to have at least a few members of my dear family among my wedding guests! Among all those people, who wished us best, nobody was a relative of mine. It was so difficult to accept the fact that I was alone, and though I was starting a family with a person I loved, deep inside me, I was weeping inconsolably. This condition would accompany me all the rest of my life during all the joyful family events I was ever granted to experience. No matter how happy and proud I would be with all the religious events within my growing family, my children, grandchildren and great-grandchildren that God was to bless me with, a part of me deep inside never stopped weeping. I was unable to overcome that yearning for the family I had lost, my dear brothers and sisters. I regretted my parents were not given the chance to know my own children and to learn that their family tree was growing, despite all the traps the Nazis made to cut it down completely, to prevent its branches from growing.

Now I was going to the holy city of Jerusalem, where I was about to spend a honeymoon with my newlywed wife at the hotel Babad. It was the present from the owner, my wife's relative. After the six years of horror, it was a dream come true for me. If before, during those harsh moments, somebody had told me that my life would turn the way it did, it would have been completely unimaginable for me. All I was thinking about was to survive the next minute, not to die of hunger, not to be hit. I was so grateful now for the beautiful moments I was sharing with my wife, for the gift of the new, safe life I was granted to start.

Although I had only six pounds in my wallet in the beginning of my marriage, we were calm, satisfied, and thankful for what fate had brought to us. We lived temporarily in the flat we had and tried to eke out our living through any possible means. I brought my wife sandwiches and canned beef that we ate together; we sold used bottles back to stores and bought potatoes in return. It was a simple and calm life, and everybody was living that way; times were not easy, but people were not giving up in spirit, especially the survivors, for whom such conditions were a kind of paradise regained after what we had left behind.

Soon the army apartment in Tel Aviv was ready, and we moved there, starting our new life. I rented the previous one to a friend's daughter, which provided me with an amount of money and made it easier to live. Friends were always around with their helping hands; when my wife became tired of the grayness of our tiles, I went to the factory where I used to work and a manager was happy to give me, "such a brave soldier," a 40 percent discount for white, shiny floor tiles with a beautiful pattern. A unit commander from Zrifin helped me with his truck, and I carried the material up. Thank God, I was strong.

Most of our neighbors were the officers I knew from the clinics where I worked. They willingly offered their help, which all the dwellers used when we needed some assistance during everyday life. We knew and trusted one another. Since there was no bus transport at that time, and rarely could anybody afford a car, we encountered small obstacles when had to leave the place in need. In such moments, for example, we asked one another for babysitting. I also had my own function in that support system. I used to be a local medic, giving injections and dressing wounds. I must admit I didn't feel comfortable treating women, but I did not want to refuse them. It would have caused them trouble being forced to travel in search of a doctor. Again, I witnessed deep appreciation from all those I helped and could always count on them in return. We lived a peaceful, quiet life in our small community, trying to make our lives calm and happy. Interestingly enough, one of the inhabitants of this district was Shimon Peres[1], whom I used to meet in the synagogue and whose children used to attend the same religious school with my children.

All this was my new life on Peace Road, 113 Derech Ha'*Shalom*, where I started my new life. My wife was already nine months pregnant at that

---

1   Shimon Peres, the ninth President of the State of Israel, twice before serving as its Prime Minister, laureate of Nobel Peace Prize together with Yitzhak Rabin and Yasser Arafat for peace talks he participated in

time. The name of our street, together with the fact of a coming new life we had created, was highly meaningful and symbolic for me. After all these dramatic separations and the death that surrounded me, after all the inner and outer fights and struggles, Fate finally was to bless me with peace and calmness, replacing my painful loses with creation.

My first baby was born in 1953. A girl. There was not a happier man in the universe when she was born. I had to be in the army, at that time, but was phoning Meir Hospital in Kfar Saba almost every hour to check the situation, and asking the nurse not to forget to let me know if anything happened in the meantime. My wife, deeply touched, later confessed to me, "I knew it would be a girl. Your mother was in my dream. She blessed me." I looked at her, stunned and with a tight throat, unable to say a word. It was the second time I heard about my mother from my wife, who had never had a chance to meet her. We had chosen the name for her yet even before; it was obvious she would be Lea, after my dear mother. Now I felt her approval and acceptance, however unbelievable it may seem.

Each day I used to open my eyes to make sure what I had was not a dream. Each day I thanked God, grateful in my heart, for each beautiful moment I was experiencing, for giving me an opportunity to build a family, for replacing destruction in my life with creation. The birth of Lea brought yet even more gratitude and appreciation that I felt. I cherished every moment I had with her, each filling me with the joy and love I had forgotten during the cruel Nazi regime. My thankfulness was so deep that every day I used to write down the beautiful moments she gave us, which for others may have seemed so obvious and common.

In 1954 came another girl, Shoshana, carrying the name after my dear grandmother from my mother's side. In 1958 God blessed us with a son and we gave him a name after my dear father, Yoseph. Quite a time after that, as late as in 1970, another boy came, and we decided he would carry the name after my beloved younger brother, Zvi (Hirsh). They all filled my life with happiness and pride.

Now, after so many years, I am sitting in the concentration camp of Auschwitz after an emotional day. I look at all of them, equally touched and supportive. In my heart I thank God again that I was given time to live until that moment, to survive the unimaginable exhaustion of body and spirit, to come out of numerous traps and start my own family, who would bring me so much happiness and become such help in my never ending process of returning to life.

I am looking at the place and wonder again how I made it, and how I finally left it. I recall the icy cold winter of 1945, as we, poor, skinny beings gathered together outside, shaking feebly due to emaciation and freezing wind. We were to leave the camp, according to the order.

EIGHT

At the end of 1944, rumors of camp liquidations started to reach us more often. Here and then we heard voices of approaching Russians, of the end of the war, of German surrender. In the distance we could hear cannons. Was it true?

Finally, after a few weeks of expectations, changes came to our camp. One day in cold, snowy winter of January 1945, they gathered thousands of us and led out of the camp, without explaining too much. There we went, into the open space, yet still guarded by the Nazis. We kept walking through forests and fields. It was a depressing and miserable sight. We were weak and weary bodies with hollow, fearful faces, shaking in the temperature of - 20 degrees Celsius. We still wore rags that barely covered our skinny bodies and clogs on our swollen feet. Wooden shoes gave us no warmth but brought about suffering, due to their shape causing numerous blisters and wounds to our feet. There was no food or drink for us. It was a challenge to endure those inhumane cruelties. Many died of exhaustion; many were helped with shots from our torturers who would not wait or have any mercy. Whoever slowed down, stopped, or could not continue was immediately killed. The blood from the murdered stained the white path we were walking. Nazis did not tolerate any delay. They rushed and hastened us all the way. How long was it going to last? I began to feel pain in my feet from the uncomfortable shoes, the cold and the general exhaustion. I tried to hide among others, so I would not be noticed limping. I desperately wanted to stay alive. If I had survived until now, all those years, I did not want to lose my life in, what seemed to be, the last stages of the war.

We kept walking in the freezing temperature, wet and trembling. Fierce wind howled into our faces and hit us with sharp snowflakes. "Shneller!" we heard all the time. Hundreds of us must have died on the way. The rest of us, after three days, which for us seemed all ages, arrived in the Mauthausen camp. We had reached Austria. In time, historians would name these tremendously brutal walks "the death marches," due to the enormous death toll they took. The Nazis, knowing already that they had lost their war, were dragging the remaining prisoners out of camps and taking us further west, toward the Reich. They wanted to prevent the truth of the camps and genocide from coming out; therefore, while they were escaping, they were also trying to destroy the traces of their deeds. For that same reason, they would take us away from the liberators. We were witnesses, who could speak out of what we had seen and experienced in their camps. We could confirm and describe the procedures of exterminating people in gas chambers and burning them in crematoria.

Yet so many of us died on the way! People were virtually falling every few meters. We left their dead bodies behind like signs marking our path in blood.

How I survived, I don't know.

In Mauthausen, they placed us in the barracks that were empty. They did not have any specific work for us there. Their only aim was to keep humiliating us. They were good at it! They came up with countless derisive activities. One day after breakfast, they took us to a big room, made us sit on the floor and take our shirts off. "You are now to find all the lice in your clothes and kill it with your thumbnails," we heard. "I am going to come back in a few hours and check carefully. Should I find one, tiny louse, you will be dead!"

So we sat for hours and tried to kill all that was walking on us. However ridiculous it seemed, we knew they meant what they said. At times they picked a few of us, handed us toothbrushes, and told us to clean the floors spotless; at times we had to transfer sand from one pile to the other, using tiny containers. Once we finished, we had to bring it back again. We did the same with bags of dirt. Did it make no sense? Oh it made sense: it made us as low as possible, to get rid of any remains of self-esteem we might still have lurking inside. They also took care we would not remain idle while we died a slow death.

Time passed slowly. We spent most of it in tents, counting off the days that had gone. After a few such weeks, which could be two months in reality, yet even weaker and thinner, we were marched again to another camp. We wished it would finally be over; we felt changes were coming. Were we going to welcome them? How long could we sustain it? Thank God, I was still alive, after coming so close to dying so many times, but was I still going to be alive the next day?

This next time our death march took us only one day. We made it in around eight hours. We were fortunate that it was no longer and that we managed it. Even eight hours meant superhuman effort for our emaciated and tired bodies. We arrived in Gunskirchen, a camp in the middle of the forest with simple barracks of no facilities. There were no beds, only ragged blankets. We were crammed inside, over two thousand people. It was impossible to lie down in such a cramped space. We were standing and leaning against one another. It was difficult to breathe. The air was becoming stuffier and stuffier. Emaciated and anguished, additionally suffering from the lack of air, people slowly slumped down, onto the others. With three of my friends, I decided to make a provisory tent among the trees, where we could try to lie down and get some sleep. Germans were no longer paying so much attention to us. They were apprehensive about what was coming, and they kept quite a distance from us, giving us more freedom in that way. There was no Capo to beat us for any slight movement or breaking the night silence, as in Auschwitz or Plaszow. Thus, we took a few blankets and tied them to branches. In this way, we built a simple shelter, which gave us more space and air. We lay down next to each other to try to get some warmth and fall asleep.

Outside it was raining. "It's not rain," I said to my companions. "Heaven is crying." We felt so sad and miserable. Was there anybody out there up above who would finish our anguish? How much longer was it going to last? What else would we have to endure?

All of us were waiting for liberation. It must have been close, judging by everything that was happening around. However, we feared that we would not be able to experience it ourselves, as we were getting thinner and weaker extremely fast now. I myself stopped feeling hunger. I virtually forced myself to swallow anything. At times I didn't even feel bothered to claim my ration. No wonder I was the weakest of my friends. They felt they had to act. They forced me to go with them. "You need to eat! Eat as much as possible!" they kept saying, worried about me. They literally dragged me with them and forced me to eat anything. I am grateful to them for that.

People reacted differently to the overwhelming hunger. Of our two thousand people, most were Hungarian Jews; we, the Polish, made up approximately two-hundred-and fifty. The Hungarians looked much better than we did; for them the real war had started just a year before! Nazis had started to bring them in as late as in 1944, which had saved them five years of profound starvation and degradation. Yet, stronger as they were, they were completely lost and helpless in dealing with the hunger. In the two last camps, I saw what true hunger is. People often say, "I am hungry," but they do not understand the meaning of these words. The hunger we experienced made us all change our understanding of food and eating. With slow degradation and malnutrition, we stole, we begged, we licked plates and desperately searched the place for any crumbs; everything became food for us.

One day a few of my comrades, completely shocked, ran to me. "Mendel, come, you won't believe it!" they managed to stutter out. "Hungarians are eating dead people!" I felt completely depressed and disheartened. So this is what we reached; this is where we had come. We had started to treat each other as objects to consume. Is there any deeper hunger that can overtake a human? I did not want to see this sad scene. Poor victims - they could not endure any more. They were simply cutting off fragments of dead bodies sprawled around and eating them. The madness of hunger must have driven them to this extreme, no doubt. I felt pure compassion for them. It would not be easy for them to live with such memories, should they survive. The Nazis had won their war, I thought, at least on humane level. We had become robots, our bodies dominated by pure instincts, our minds set on survival strategies.

The horror continued. Inside the new barracks, the weakest fainted and slowly died, lying and sleeping on each other. Oftentimes, only in the morning would someone discover the comrade lying on or under his own body had already died. Growing weaker every minute, people had not enough strength to move either the dead bodies or themselves aside; they simply continued lying or sleeping on each other.

I myself felt I was getting weaker day by day. One day, while lying in a tent, I felt so miserable and feeble I knew I was going to faint. The place seemed to be deprived of any air. It was densely populated with trees, which themselves hardly put any wind inside. To make things worse, the area was slowly filling with the odors of decaying bodies, some lying somewhere around, and some dug under the ground. Nazis ordered to bury the dead, but since we were extremely weak and the number of the dead was constantly growing, we could not manage with cleaning the ground. Too weak to do anything else, we slept there, relieved ourselves there, and died there. We hadn't truly washed ourselves for a long time. I dreamt of water to refresh my face, maybe to drink a little, but there was none. I looked up, but even the sky was dry, as if it had already poured down all its tears and could not help me.

One of my friends looked at me and said with hesitation, "There is a pool right here, but it's too dangerous to go there. It is next to Nazi location."

"I don't care what will happen, I need to go there and come to my senses," I said, very determined.

My comrades looked at one another helplessly. "You can't go alone. You are too weak," they decided, and one of them was ready to accompany me. We left, the two of us, risking our lives.

It was true. The pool was very close, but because of my weakness and dizziness, it seemed like kilometers. But what a relief it was to lie down and sprinkle our faces and bodies with water! It removed some of our tiredness and resignation. I felt I was coming back to my senses. We felt much better and slowly made our way back. We did not even manage to sit down when we came back, when we heard Nazis yelling their orders: "Stand in line! Everyone form a pair!" I got scared. What could that mean? I quickly grabbed someone and stood as the first pair. What was going on? What were they planning? Was it some punishment? My mind was going mad with fear and, to make things worse, I was standing in the first row.

Suddenly, we saw a truck coming, but it had a big red sign. It was the Red Cross! The truck entered into the camp, and it must have been allowed by the Nazis to come, judging by their reaction. People got out of the car and opened the back door. They came with food. We couldn't believe it! They started to unload the parcels. Each of us was to run quickly, grab a package, and come back to the tent! Inside each parcel, there was a true treasure. I felt like crying. When was the last time I saw such things? We all had already forgotten what real food could mean! We all had forgotten the taste long time ago. Now, we were looking at our treasurers. Wasn't it a dream? I will forever remember exactly the items, their amounts, and tastes. Sliced Swiss cheese, sliced bread, a piece of hard jam, and even a piece of cake! It was a true feast for our famished bodies. Obviously, we couldn't eat that much. Our stomachs would not sustain it. They had to learn to digest anew. Though these were small portions in fact, it sufficed for over a week to feed us. Moreover, we were also given small packets of vitamins, which were supplements providing all necessary ingredients for body functions. We could do without food for some time by eating one or two of these.

The Red Cross visitors gave us the precious parcels and left. Since I had this package, I did not claim my camp rations as such. I sometimes took bread, sometimes margarine and tea or coffee. For the next week or two, I lay in the tent most of the time. All around, the pile of dead bodies was growing. Some of our comrades were not careful enough and died of eating too much too quickly. Every day there were those whose bodies could not endure anymore. I was resigned and weaker day by day too. One such usual day, I suddenly realized there was something wrong. My senses were teased by an incredible smell coming from the eating place. I could not believe it! Was it my imagination? It had been months since they had given us a warm meal, and the water that they called cabbage or turnip soup had never had such smell! But yes, someone was cooking food, and it kept luring with its aromas promising us, famished skeletons, real satiation.

Why was this happening? Was a change taking place after the Red Cross visit? Is it the end of the war? People did not wait, they did not think. The hunger drove them after the smell, and they ran blindly to the source of the powerful scent. I was so sad that I could not join them. I was too weak. I could not even stand up. I so wished I could taste it! I wondered if there was enough for everybody to eat at least a little. Obviously, as I found out later, the strongest reached the place first and ate more; these were mainly Hungarians, who still were much better than us. I remained where I was, disappointed I could not join this feast.

A few moments later, the situation around me started changing dramatically.

I looked around and saw skinny bodies sprawled around, tossing and turning in convulses, moaning, and holding their stomachs! What was going on? I saw people vomiting, some coming down with diarrhea. Had they eaten too much, and their stomachs could not sustain it? I didn't know what to think!

Soon it became very clear. It couldn't be that beautiful. A real meal? For us? We must have been truly naïve. Instead, it was the last trick from our tormenters. The soup was poisoned. After so much suffering, such long years of deprivation and cruelties that these young people experienced in all the camps, they met such a malicious death in the last moments of this needless, cruel war.

In the meantime, our horror seemed to be coming to a long awaited and expected end. Suddenly, we saw our tormentors dropping their weapons in great haste and escaping from the camp. That must mean the liberating forces were approaching, we all thought. Why did not any of those who knew how to use guns lift a few and shoot our captors dead, I wondered? But who was using their common sense at that time? Who knew what truly was happening and what was coming? Also, we were too scared and intimidated. Instead, what was more understandable, people rushed to the storage rooms where they rummaged around in desperate search for food. To their happiness, they managed to find some remains, tubs of margarine and different cans. Poor creatures, fighting to get anything for themselves, stuffing their pockets, looking for tools to open the cans, escaping with their treasures, snatching them from one another - all for nothing. All to meet the same end as those who had yielded to the tempting soup trap before, since these products were poisoned as well.

I cried bitter tears. The view of my comrades dying with such convulsions such unnecessary death, was infinitely depressing. I thought I could not sustain anything more. The method the Nazis chose was incomprehensibly cruel and at the same time truly shrewd. Even though we were convinced nothing could surprise or shock us anymore after all we had experienced so far, their last trap came to us all completely unexpected, and we found it beyond understanding. To lure famished, emaciated bodies with warm, soothing liquid... who would resist it? I myself so much regretted I couldn't be there to alleviate a little of my aching, empty stomach.

I looked at this sad sight realizing it was yet another time that I had been saved. Had I been strong enough to move my body, I would have been lying there with my companions, suffering and dying. It was yet another blessing in disguise. I could not comprehend it. It was clear that despite all the suffering I had gone through, somebody had cared for me by saving me from Death's arms, taking me to safer places. Although at times I rebelled, it always used to prove the end was good and meant to help me. What seemed to me injustice in the beginning, with time gained a meaning of a sign that I was guided to safe places and protected from traps. Was there any deeper meaning in that?

I was lying inside the blanket tent, exhausted physically and mentally. I became a Musulman, as they would call us - a skinny, shadowy figure, not dead yet, but no longer alive, one of the walking skeletons, all looking the same. I didn't know if I would be able to face more than I had so far. Fortunately, I did not have to; our long, hoped-for day arrived. The years of torment was coming to an end. I could not be truly happy, however, despite deep relief. I was too weak. The view around me reminding me of the last scenes was not helpful either. My fateful companions who, only hours ago were waiting with me for this moment, were dead, their skinny bodies sprawled on the ground, their faces still distorted in pain. Some had died of poisoned food; some of putting too much to their stomachs, which a long time ago had forgotten their functions; some had simply given up. What was there for me? Did I have any chances of regaining strength at all?

My thinking was disturbed by the voices of coming people. Those of my companions who were able to move themselves left, running to meet the liberators, to look for food and clothes in the surrounding villages, to feel the first moments of freedom. I did not have that strength. I did not find enough of it even to answer the doctors who came to me. They tried hard to make their way both through densely sprawling trees and bodies. They checked carefully to see who in the piles was dead, who agonized, who was still alive. We had not been given food or water since the Germans had left two days before, and before then, the rations had gotten smaller. We were, skeletons covered with skin, rags, and vermin. We lay together exhausted and not sure ourselves which of our neighbors were dead and which alive. I saw the doctors were deeply touched with what they saw.

One of them who was Jewish spoke to me in Yiddish.

"We will now examine you," he explained. They put me on the scales and it showed sixty-two pounds, twenty-eight kilograms approximately. I was a twenty-one-year-old man and weighed less than thirty kilograms. They looked at each other helplessly.

"Look, my friend," the doctors continued. "We are sorry, but we cannot help you, because of the state you are in. You have a few more hours of living ahead of you, maybe days. We, of course, will not leave you here and will give you a proper treatment in the hospital. We are taking you now to Wels, to the hospital. But please remember, if by any chance you survive and recover, it will not be due to our proficiency. It will be a miracle from above, from God."

I did remember. I had enough time for thinking in the hospital, where I spent a few months before I was well enough to leave it. I tried to embrace these long almost six years of horror and all that happened to me. I was virtually torn out of the safe life I had with my family in my hometown, Szczekociny. One day it turned out we, the Jewish nation, were the worst enemies of Germans, and there was no place for us in the new world they were trying to build. I was a completely different human now the war was over. I thought about all the miracles I experienced during that time. Yes, these were all miracles from God, I was sure. Otherwise I would have been dead a long time ago. Images ran through my head. I remembered my father ordering me to go with my younger brother, which led us out of the Wodzislaw ghetto. I recalled a Nazi pulling my brother off the truck, to our deep sorrow. Painful corporal punishment for stealing bread. Typhoid fever in Plaszow Gulag I, when I was sure I would die, like the final 80 percent of the camp. *Yom Kippur* in Plaszow II, when I was standing in front of bullets being shot at me. Jumping out of the death train to Auschwitz. Two Germans driving me off to prison in their car. Hernia operation in Auschwitz. Death marches to Mauthausen and Gunskirchen. Food poisoning. And now, the words of the doctors that I had only a few hours more.

Well, indeed, the nurses taking care of me complained: "It is easier to look after a pre-mature born baby, a fetus in an incubator, than to treat you," they said. "So many years of our profession and we had never seen people your age with their bones protruding from everywhere and no skin!"

I, on the other hand, was surprised at how the voice could sound, and what emotions it could to create. The voices of the nurses brought me back the forgotten world. I found the way they spoke, so soft and gentle, almost unnatural. I had to slowly get used to it again, learning back with pleasure at the sound of true human talking. How soothing it was to listen to them! What a piece of mind I could sustain, how calm my heartbeats could be, my body no longer paralyzed with panic inflicted with hateful yelling and shouting. I was again talked to, I was not expected to stand upright, and I did not have to cower inside under the loud, heavy yelling.

I was making it. Another miracle. All these events had made me a different person. They had made me realize nothing is certain, nothing is doomed, and though life is so fragile and we can lose it at any time, there is some deeper meaning and some stronger powers in our existence. Life is a greater mystery than any of us could imagine.

In my mind, I returned to the first days of the war, when we lived in the ghetto. It seemed difficult at that time, yet compared to what I had experienced in the camps, it was quite a decent life there. I was deeply convinced of one thing. Even through the fear, death risk, threats, limited food, and other cruelties from the hands of our tormentors, we would have survived. Had they lasted even ten or fifteen years, we would have made it. It wasn't the first time we, the Jewish, were taken captive, tormented, persecuted, hated, and forced to hard labor. The Bible had taught us our history. Yet, for the first time in the history of our nation, we were simply being exterminated. Babies, children, women and elderly alike. *Endlosung*, as they called it. Their main aim was to annihilate our entire nation and our culture. The fact that they carefully burned utterly our bodies, destroyed our holy books, and all signs of our religion, and razed our synagogues and cemeteries to the ground, as well as their derisive words: "We will tell the world the history of the camps," leads me to a bitter conclusion. Not only was there no place for us in the world they were trying to build, but they wanted to erase us from its history.

Had they won, had they managed to burn us all, what would have happened within next years, and decades? We witnessed the shaping of history and, thank God, the outcome was different from what they had planned, though they managed to bring about so much suffering and destruction and made us all change our thinking of humanity.

The German nation, associated with the highest art, culture, and standards, shocked the whole world with six years of meticulously planned terror aimed at those whom they found unworthy of carrying the name of a human and threatening their new order of *Ubermensch* [1]; especially Jews, but also Roma, Baltic and Slavic nations, handicapped, and homosexuals. Only the west, as Nazi believed, could create true culture; therefore, all intellectuals in Poland became their enemies too, and ended in concentration camps.

I lay in bed thinking, watching soldiers incessantly bringing survivors, all of whom looked more or less like me. It took some time, but there came the day when I could leave the hospital on my own legs. I could thank the doctors and nurses for their care and go outside. I was free. The war was over. At the same time, I was completely alone. What should I do now?

---

1   *Ubermensch*, German, "Overman", "Superman", a concept in the philosophy of Friedrich Nietzche, used in a perverted way by Nazis

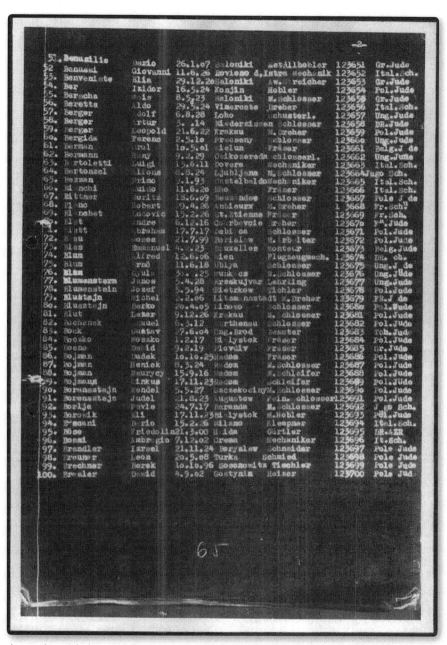

A copy of an original transport list created by authorities in Mauthausen noting arrivals on 29 January 1945. Mendel Borensztajn's name appears on line number 90 of this list. This list provides Mendel Borensztajn's name, date of birth (The correct date of birth of Izyk Mendel Bornstein is 17.03.1924), place of birth, occupation, Mauathausen prisoner number, 123690, and prisoner type, Polish Jew

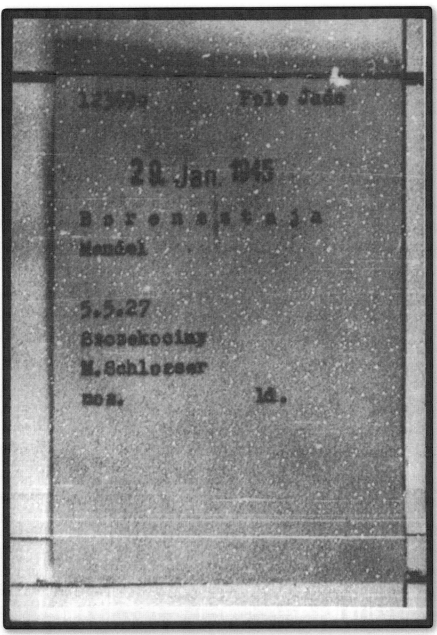

A copy of a card created by Mauthausen regarding Mendel Borensztajn. This card provides Mendel Borensztajn's name, Mauthausen prisoner number, 123690, date of arrival, 29 January 1945, date of birth, place of birth, occupation, religion as "mos.," "mosaisch," Jewish, and marital status as "ledig," single. This card was housed in the administration office at Mauthausen

A copy of an original prisoner number register created by authorities in Mauthausen. Mendel Borensztajn's name appears near the bottom of this document, next top his Mauthausen prisoner number, 123690. This register provides Mendel Borensztajn's name, date of birth, prisoner type as Polish Jew and place of birth

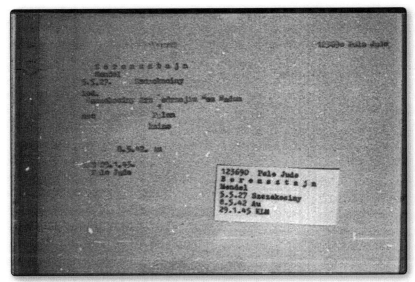

A copy of an original prisoner card created by authorities in Mauthausen regarding Mendel Borensztajn. This prisoner card displays personal information regarding Mendel Borensztajn including his date of birth, place of birth, marital status as single, pre-deportation address, date of arrival in Auschwitz, 8 May 1942, date of arrival in Mauthausen, 29 January 1945, and Mauthausen prisoner number, 123690

An additional copy of an original prisoner card created by authorities in Mauthausen regarding Mendel Borensztajn. This prisoner card displays personal information regarding Mendel Borensztajn including his date of birth, place of birth, marital status as single, pre-deportation address, date of arrival in Auschwitz, 8 May 1942, date of arrival in Mauthausen, 29 January 1945, and Mauthausen prisoner number, 123690. (According to the document at the archives in Auschwitz, however, the date of Izyk Mendel Bornstein's arrival at the Auschwitz Concentration Camp was 31 July, 1944)

Eight

A copy of the reverse side of this prisoner card, which notes Mendel Borensztajn's occupation as "Schlosser."

A copy of the envelope that was created in the postwar era by staff members at the International Tracing Service to hold Mendel Borensztajn's individual records created in Mauathausen

B O R N S T E I N   Menachem Mendel   385 935

(27)

17.5.23   Szezekooin/Pol.   isr./poln.

1.40   Gh. Wooislaw
10.42   ZAL. Julag b. Plaszow
8.43   KZ. Plaszow
1.44   AL. Pionki
6.44   Auschw. Nr. B 34
12.44 - 4.45 Mauth.   Nr. B 94
5.5.45   befr.

URO Ffm

A copy of a record of an inquiry that was previously submitted to the International Tracing Service in the postwar era by a third party seeking additional information concerning Mendel Bornstein. The information that appears on this card was supplied by this third party and cannot be verified without original documentation as evidence. (According to the document at the archives in Auschwitz, however, the date of Izyk Mendel Bornstein's arrival at the Auschwitz Concentration Camp was 31 July, 1944)

NINE

I was liberated by the American Army in Guskurchen, on May 5th, 1945. That was the physical liberation. Their arrival, which we had prayed for in our weakening hearts, forced our German tormentors to escape, and we, exhausted and emaciated beings, were taken out of the camp, mainly to different hospitals for long-term processes of convalescence, after which we would be able to try to come back to a regular life.

We, however, had lost the meaning of a normal, regular, common life. After what we had gone through, was there any regular life for us? Where? What did it mean? Where would we go and how would we live?

After the relief of long expected, and dreamt about liberation, the reality started to hit our awakening senses. Provided with food, shelter, and care, and freed from fear and intimidation, our numbness and inner deadness slowly began to go away, in return making space for pain. The truth reached our hearts and minds little by little, and we, survivors, began to suffer our realization that many of us were completely alone, with no family and homes. The first moments of liberation had made us feel lucky and special; we felt chosen to witness that moment that many had no longer believed would come. With time, we started to realize what it meant indeed, and many asked ourselves the unanswerable, painful question if it would not have been better for us had we perished on the way. Did we really deserve the epithet "fortunate?" Weren't the fortunate those who had been murdered long ago and thus saved from long years of tortures?

Facing an impossible mixture of emotions, we felt completely lost. We didn't know what to do, or how to come to terms with all those nightmares coming more and more often now, and all those memories. Should we forget? Should we try to stifle the feelings? The help we received, and were unquestionably grateful for, was material and physical. We lacked professional psychological care of our wrecked insides. Our legs were soon able to carry us further, but we were not ready for that mentally or emotionally. We had to cry out our long suppressed fear, bewilderment, and shock of our experiences, and then could we try to remember slowly living behind the barbed wires and without supervision. Telling and writing down the experience we came to share, though it forced us to go through this hell again, became our cathartic process, which brought us relief. Some of us were ready for that earlier; for others, like me, it took long years before we found any sense in that process and felt ready to face our pasts.

Slowly, the big picture was revealed and the whole world learned of the atrocities perpetrated by Nazi Germany against the human race. Though wars, evil, and hatred had happened before, for the first time, and hopefully last one, the world witnessed mass extermination of certain representatives of humanity in such a short period of time and to such a great extent. For the first time, the world had to face the reality of the new order prepared by those who considered themselves a superior race. This new order was based on cold and tough rules. There was no place for the elderly, the weak or the frail; there was no place for certain civilizations, especially us, the Jewish nation. The world had to learn the facts that entire families of strong, healthy babies, children, and their mothers did not die as a direct result of the war. They had been remorselessly brought to gas chambers and burnt in crematoria. For the first time, human mind had been working hard to find yet more and more sophisticated and efficient methods of killing on a grand scale. For the first time in recorded history, the human mind had found a better use of human bodies: their fat for soap, their hair for felt and mattresses, their skin for gloves and the ash from their burnt bodies for roads. Millions of innocent lives had been wiped out from the surface of the earth.

I lost the best years of my youth. I so much regret I was not able to continue my education, to broaden my knowledge and invest in my personal development. Nazis had planned a different future for me and others alike. I had experienced a profound degradation on each level of my life: physical, mental, and spiritual.

The injuries inflicted upon my inside were much more complicated. I suspect that if there had been professional nurses taking care of this, as they took care of my body in Wels, they would have complained even more than those who complained about my physical condition. The wounds I have carried deep inside are open, aching, ineradicable. Just like the number on my left arm, they would constantly remind me of what I had gone through. These wounds are incurable, for one cannot turn back the time, which seems to be the only way to heal me and others alike - to change the past, to erase these horrible deeds, to let us never witness such unimaginable horror. I wish I had never gotten to know the feeling of losing my entire loving family, murdered for no reason in such a cruel, unthinkable manner. I wish I had not gotten to know the all-level degradation of healthy, peaceful people, the smell of burnt human bodies and the experience of starving people eating the corpses of their comrades. Could there be any return to the previous state of mind and spirit?

We were still children and adolescents when our safe worlds collapsed and we were brutally separated from our families, uncertain of what was to become of them, uncertain if we would ever be able to see them again or ever come back to our homes. We lived in the shadows of working crematoria and gas chambers, annihilating and burning the bodies of our Jewish brothers and sisters, dreading at the shudder premonition our closest relatives are sharing their fate, trying hard to stifle cruel conclusions and preserve hope against all we were witnessing around. I saw how little a human body came to mean, burnt in crematoria after careful search for any golden teeth inside their dead, gassed mouth, their ashes finally spread onto roads and treaded into the soil. Shocked and saddened, I confronted it with all the religious rules we had tried hard to preserve in our old, safe world after the death of our relatives and friends. I recalled the utmost respect we used to pay to the dead bodies before, during, and after the burial.

Fear. Constantly present, it became our faithful comrade. Only fear, together with its war brother hunger, did not fail us. It accompanied every step, wherever we moved. We felt it ceaselessly. We could never be sure we would be still alive the next moment; we could never be sure of the next step of our tormentors.

On the surface, I was fortunate to be freed from the nightmare of Holocaust; I managed to build a good life with enough to eat, a place to live in, a wife, children, and friends. Had anyone been able to see what was going on inside, however, they would have realized that my efforts to build a life in the outside world were nothing compared to the endeavors I made inside to make the pieces of my crushed inner world whole again. I never completed this mission as perfectly as what I managed to accomplish on the outside. The inner scars are thick and will stay with me all my life.

Now, accompanied by my closest family, I head back to Szczekociny, the main destination of our journey. I am a completely different person than when I left this small *shtetl* as a fifteen-year-old boy. What will I find there? How much have things changed since I last saw it on that sad day when I left it with my family?

The late summer of 1939 was the beginning of the end. The autumn was already coming. It brought with it a sad course of events; it was becoming more and more obvious that the war was imminent. August 31, 1939 was the first day I could see my life was going to change dramatically. We were one of the few families in Szczekociny who had a radio at home, so we kept up with the news, which became more and more dispiriting. Finally, it was announced one day that the Germans were approaching. We knew what it meant: the war had started. We got careful instructions to let all the Jewish community in Szczekociny know that they should move to a forest for the time of marching in the German army, which had been said to be coming closer to our *shtetl*, and then to come back when things were more or less settled. We were informed they were going to use teargas, so the order was to put duct tape around windows to prevent it from getting inside our houses. We did as we were told. We took just the minimum to survive. We knew we would be coming back within the next days, hopefully, to quite stable circumstances. Fortunately, it was still quite warm, so it was not a problem to remain outside long hours, even at night, and sleep on the ground. We took only the necessary items: pillows, blankets, towels and some food.

Bombed houses and repressed inhabitants during the Second World War in Szczekociny. The Jewish girl on the left was allegedly murdered after the picture was taken, according to the contemporary testimony of the Polish girl on the right, Ms Szczepanska (Fiodorow)

I saw many people heading anxiously in one direction for shelter. A lot of families decided to hide in the woods. I presume most of those living on main streets and apparently the majority of the Jewish community left the town for the seemingly most dangerous moments. We spent the night outside, not knowing what the next day would be like. I don't think people actually slept in the forest. We were worried, feeling that something had finished, and what was coming was far from positive. We could hear the approaching tanks and the marching troops. With all we had read in papers before and had heard on the radio about what the Nazis had been doing to the Jewish in Germany and Austria, we feared the worst. However, although we did not know what to expect, none of us ever suspected in their most dreadful nightmares the horrific magnitude of what was about to come.

We felt quite safe hidden among the trees, but we didn't sleep. When the daylight came and things seemed more secure, my father sent my older sister and me back to the town to check the situation. It was dangerous for adults to go out. Germans had no problem at all recognizing Jewish men. Long beards with *Peyes* [1] and characteristic clothes made them an easy target. We heard before of cruel and humiliating persecutions, aimed mostly at men. Their beards were remorselessly and cruelly cut to the accompaniment of disdainful laughing, beating and often picture taking. My father, whose appearance was of a typical Orthodox Jew, could risk losing his life.

Full of anxiety over what we would find there, we set off together with Rivka. The closer we were to the town centre, the more horrible the view was. It was no longer my safe environment. The streets where I had walked and run free all my childhood were now covered with dead bodies, mostly Jewish, sprawled all around. We encountered them in Senatorska Street and around the church. The houses did not look like I remembered them from hours before. Many were destroyed, with broken glass and black traces, many burnt from the bombs that ripped through the town, rained down by Germans. I was growing increasingly shocked and petrified.

Slowly, with growing fear, we approached our house. We were deeply saddened by the sight of it. It had not been saved. It was such a heartbreaking moment to see the place of our family warmth and happiness, our shelter, torn apart by invaders to whom we had not done anything wrong. One store had been completely burnt. Fortunately enough, our tenant, Leibe Goldberg, had an iron door to his shoe-shop. This not only saved the ground floor from being burnt, but it also stopped the fire from entering inside. It seemed the destruction was not that serious and after some repair works, we would be able to move back in again.

We found that many of the people who saw abandoned Jewish houses with open doors cut by bombs and fire let themselves freely inside, robbing the shops and basements. Our house inside was robbed too. After years I was told by my neighbor, Kazimiera Wojtasinska, that Nazis not only calmly watched the situation, but they actually encouraged Catholics to take whatever they wished from Jewish shops and houses. It was made clear there would be no more Jewish merchants in the town. My father, understanding the situation and realizing he would not be able to sell

---

1 *Peyes*, Hebrew, "sides" or "edges", sidelocks worn by religious Orthodox Jews, as a practice of Jewish law regarding shaving

anymore of his merchandise, came to Kazimiera's mother after that time and invited her to take some of his goods too. It was better, as he felt it, to give it to the friendly neighbors instead of letting it be stolen or destroyed. She, however, a decent woman, was literally indignant with that offer: "To take my neighbor's belongings? Never!"

Although it was a difficult situation, neither my father nor any of us were too much or too long saddened by the stealing. In a moment like that, we were just happy that we stayed alive.

I was not prepared for the atrocities I saw in the town. Were these sights and experiences appropriate for a boy my age? Destroyed houses, people robbing the basements, empty streets, dead bodies sprawling around, smoke, and tanks; fear and sadness heavily poisoning the stifling atmosphere. And above all, our new inhabitants were those nobody had invited to our calm and lovely town, and who definitely had not come with friendly intentions. What would now become of us all? Was our world finished? When would they go? It felt like a terrible nightmare. All of a sudden, our peaceful lives came to an end and our childhood unnaturally finished.

How quickly everything could radically change, literally turning the old, well-known world upside down. It was still the same town, yet it was completely different. People were no longer the same either. They were scared and nervous. Some were already dead, yet others turned into enemies robbing the possessions of neighbors. Everything had changed everything changed during the night with the invasion of that brutality to our safe, calm lives. Was it irreversible? Would it go back to what we had known before?

In the meantime, Rivka and I kept entering different houses hiding for a while. We feared to go back to the streets, which were full of German tanks and military vehicles. We realized the situation was serious, and we were no longer safe in our town. Even more, we could no longer trust all our neighbors. Scared and dispirited, we continued vigilantly looking for our family, friends, and other well-known faces. Were they all right? We managed to talk to a few people and then we came back to the forest and told our parents what we had just seen. They became truly alarmed.

Nevertheless, they decided to come back to the town. We couldn't stay forever in a forest.

After a few days, the situation became more settled. My father hired professionals to put a wooden roof over the shop so that we would have a place to live. We had no other choice but to grow accustomed to the new circumstances. Germans demanded from the head of the community a list of Jewish families in the town. They began to control our lives. They required each day one member of the family to come up and work, which must have been a proof for them that the family remained in Szczekociny. I went every day, instead of my father, and I worked usually with farming. I didn't want my father to take any risk. The persecutions had started already in our small town. Some people saw Germans cut the beards of Jews. They did not care enough to check if they cut only hair; they deliberately aimed at tearing the skin as well. It seemed to bring them more satisfaction. They did not hesitate to kill some poor victims either. I tried not to attract any unnecessary attention from the Nazis.

Szczekociny's Market Place (Rynek) during the Second World War

Szczekociny's Market Place and houses that were destroyed during bombing in the Second World War. In the centre, the synagogue with destroyed roof, next to it visible walls of the old Jewish cemetery

After two months, more or less, of uncertain days and deteriorating conditions, we were unexpectedly visited by three Germans. They looked around and said cynically, "What a lovely shop. You have eight days to get out of here." We were deeply saddened by this order. To get out where? Why? To leave what my parents earned with hard work and what we cherished so much all those years? It was devastating news for us. However, my father kept reassuring us: "There is nothing more precious than life."

They were already creating a ghetto for Jews. We were to live in a separate district, to leave our homes and move into what they specified for us in the tiny area of three streets in the center[1]. It was too cramped; therefore, my father decided it would be better to move to Wodzislaw, his hometown. He still had a house there from his father, from the period before he married my mother and moved to Szczekociny. Perhaps we would be safer there, we all hoped. Before we left, my dear father had asked me to follow him to a place

1   These days they are the streets of Sciegiennego, Krakowska and Wesola

where he wanted to tell me something important. "Remember this place," he said, as if knowing I was the one to survive of all our family. "Here I had hidden our most precious family valuables with our pictures." I looked at his serious face and with a tight throat nodded my head. I hoped he would be the one to take them back again to the daylight, and we all would be relieved that everything ended well. Perhaps, I kept wondering later in my life, my father had known more than he was telling and showing us.

Having hired a cart with two horses, and we set off on our difficult journey. Of course, it was very difficult for us to leave our lovely house, with all we had inside, and our hometown, where we had lived such a happy life. We did not know when or if we would be able to come back here again. Our hearts were torn apart, but we had to stay alive. Our lives were more important than anything else and our family was most precious. We took the most necessary things for everyday life and my parents, my younger brother, my two sisters, and me left. It was the cold winter of January 1940. That was also the last time I would be inside my dear house.

Now, after sixty years, I wonder if it is standing there still? Did it survive the war times and bombings? Is there anybody living inside? Did any our personal possessions survive? Did somebody use them? My mind is full of thoughts and questions, my heart full of apprehension.

On the way, we stop in the nearby Lelov, once a meaningful Jewish community, a place of birth and living of Rabbi David Biderman[1], one of the most important centers of the *Chassidic* movement in Poland. Now we see an empty town with Jewish houses but now inhabited 100 percent by Christians. We find the entrance to the place of Biderman's eternal rest. To our amazement, it is now located at the back of the shop. Only the door with the Star of David marks this holy place. We are saddened by the disappearance of cemeteries and these buildings built on top of them. We are told the descendants of Rabbi Biderman bought this place to facilitate the annual arrivals of *Chassidim* to pray at his grave. We light candles and say prayers there too, which comes as a kind of comfort after the

---

1   Rabbi David Biderman, from the Lelover dynasty, a disciple of the Seer of Lublin, a spiritual leader for *Chassidim*, his maxims and thoughts are well known and cited all over the world; his grave is visited each year by religious *Chassidic* Jews

dreadful experience of Auschwitz. In a tiny, nearby hut, we find the two hundred-year-old *Mykve*, where local religious Jews used to come and purify themselves before religious festivals. It is not used anymore, serving different purposes. There is a private flat, but still one can see a hanger for coats inside.

I think about the *Mykve* and the two cemeteries in Szczekociny. What will I find there? What conditions are they in? The closer we get, the more excited and at the same time apprehensive I become. Finally, we reach the place, and my heart is beating faster. Here I am, at the place I thought I would never see again. Here, where I was born, where I grew up so happy. My mind is full of images and memories, my heart filled with overwhelming emotions. I have returned.

TEN

Szczekociny. I get out of the car, and we start walking around. I don't recognize much. Everything seems completely different. We go to the main market square, and now I feel home. I am standing next to the monument of Kosciuszko! It has been renovated, and I am certain it was once facing a different direction (which with time will be confirmed.) Now I am truly touched. It used to be a much calmer and more peaceful place. I presume there are no more people coming and selling their goods on a market day here. There is simply no space. Rynek now has become very colorful and noisy; cars are going all the time around; and it is cut in half by a busy road. I look at the Jewish houses surrounding the place. I vaguely remember where some shops used to be. There are still shops, but I presume they are not Jewish. Do any Jews live here, behind these old Jewish walls?

I want to see my house. We meet an elderly man and ask him about Sienkiewicza Street. "It used to be such a street here once," he answers, "but they have changed its name and I don't remember where it used to be." I describe the exact location to him, saying it can't be difficult to find, due to the fact it was next to the only church in this small town. Now he knows where to take us. We keep walking for a while and turn the main street right. Suddenly, I see the church! It means this is the street! How much everything changed though, I hardly recognize the buildings. They look completely different, bigger and more colorful. After a moment I am sure I found it. This is my house! It looks completely different, but the number is still the same, though the street is now Koscielna. The number is still seven. I am overwhelmed with emotions. I see there is a shop too, and people are living inside. I stand in front of it, and the images come back.

We used to live on the top floor, in three spacious rooms. There was also one large room with a separate entrance and a beautiful balcony overlooking the street. It had iron railings painted black, where you could place flowers and plants. However, this room did not belong to us; my parents rented it to a dentist. One of its walls was adjacent to our first room, and its uppermost part was made of clear and unbreakable glass.

Inside the room next to the dentist's, behind the sliding door, there were our

Ten

beds on the left side, whereas the right wall was covered with shelves that held textile merchandise for tailors in wholesale. These were materials my father used to bring for his shop. In the middle of the room there was a table for fabric measurement. Instead of the fourth wall, there was a huge five foot wide tile stove, stretching from the floor up to the ceiling and covered with porcelain. It had a small iron door on its lower part, through which we placed logs to warm the house. It could keep warmth even up to two and a half days! In my mind's eye I see people coming inside during cold winter days and immediately rushing to the stove with their hands close to its walls, getting warmth as much as they could, and appreciating the bright white porcelain.

The living room had two cabinets on the left wall, which separated two beds belonging to my parents. The right wall had a large window consisting of three panes. Next to the entrance to the kitchen, there was a large mirror that slanted slightly, so that you could see yourself from top to bottom, and three round stools around twenty-five centimeters in diameter. In the middle, there was a shelf of around twenty centimeters for flowerpots. In the middle of the room, there was a long, oval-shaped table with twelve chairs around. Try as you might, even with the sharpest knife, you could never scratch its surface. During the weekdays, it was covered with a flowery thick tablecloth; on *Shabbat* and holidays we spread a white flowery one. Over the table, there was a heavy brass lamp hanging from the ceiling that lit this long room.

I remember all the details. I close my eyes and I can tell the surface, the colors, and the sizes of apparently all the items we had inside. It is as if my heart took a picture of them. One day we had to leave everything. One day, all that we had taken care of and cherished for many years, stayed inside our beloved home and we were forced to go.

I can hear the steps of my mother and Sara, who would now and then climb stairs to the attic. They would hang the laundry out there and then bring it down. I remember the smell of my washed clothes, soaked with the characteristic smell of the attic, and of the straw, which was spread on the floor to keep the warmth.

I look down. Here, we had the same amount of rooms as upstairs, and a store; however, this part was taken by Leibe Goldberg and his wife, Sheindel, my parents' tenants. They used to live with us for almost thirty years, until the outbreak of the war. They had a big store for shoes, furs, fabrics, and materials. Almost every house had a sewing machine, and many women would come here, interested in their materials, mostly for sheets and bedclothes, as at that time mothers used to sew them for their daughters before these got married.

All in all, it was a very big and spacious house. That enabled us to hold weddings there on Saturday evenings, after *Shabbat*. Many friends of ours would ask my parents for help in organizing their wedding parties. We would open all the doors between the rooms to make one huge space. Musicians and comedians would come to entertain guests. We all used to have so much joy! Then, the house was filled with merry voices, stomping of feet on the wooden floor, clinking of glasses and cutlery, and obviously, wonderful smells of tasty dishes. I still remember the violinist's name; it was Leibel Pastecki.

Next to the house we lived in, there was another wooden one. In the front part of it, Chaim Yoseph Rafaelowicz's widow used to live with her two daughters. We did not charge her a rent. She only paid taxes. She tried hard to make her living in a grocery store she used to run. The back part of the house we rented to David Zuckerman. He lived there in a large room with his wife and son. He also used his place as a shop, where he produced the top parts of shoes. Trading was the most popular way of earning a living among Jews those days.

I wonder what is now behind the house. I remember the yard outside stretched up to a narrow street. There was a beautiful, green wooden gate for a horse and a wagon, and a small wicket gate to enter. In the garden, we had two wooden buildings that we used as warehouses. There was also our yearly *Sukkah* [1], a kind of open hut, which had a manually operated roof in case of rain. Thus, even if it was wet, we were able to go and eat outside.

---

1   *Sukkah*, Hebrew, from a word denoting the material for building, "a hut" or a "booth", a temporary dwelling used by Jews during the festival of *Sukkoth* mainly for eating of meals, also for sleeping, in warmer countries, during the time of the festival

The Goldberg family, who used to be our tenants, always joined us for the holiday. We were dressed in our best, holiday clothes as we sat around the table with a flowery tablecloth, silverware and candles burning in the evening. We would eat delicious food and freshly baked *Challah*, and my father would bring refined wine, such as Malaga. Funny, I even remember the plates we used at that time, they were very thin and elegant with three golden lines around. We used to sit there and eat our meals with all the family during *Sukkoth* [1]. Do these new owners also enjoy now sitting there, in the garden?

I remember everything so well. It brings so much pain to realize I can stand here and wait endlessly, yet I will not see my parents or siblings going out. It is very difficult to accept the fact my home, my shelter, where I was born and brought up, was taken over by other people who live there happily now, without, perhaps, paying too much attention what happened to its first owners. I wonder if any pictures survived the fire and bombing. I am not so much interested in any material objects, but pictures of my beloved family would be a treasure. I did not take anything with me when leaving this place.

Maybe by another miracle there is at least one photograph that survived and would reach me, just as the book of my beloved father did? I remember how shocked I was when one day, around twenty years after the war, my wife's nephew visited me. That day deeply touched and thrilled me. Dudi Silbershlag is an ultra-orthodox media personality, and his favorite hobby while growing up used to be collecting old books, especially Jewish ones. That day, he came with The Examination of the World by Rabbi Jedaiah ben Abraham Bedersi. He handed me the book, pointing at its first page with Hebrew handwriting: "For God is the land and its fullness. Belongs to Yoseph Hanoch Borensztajn".

---

1   *Sukkoth*, Hebrew, the Feast of Tabernacles, celebrated on the fourteenth day of the month *Tishrei*, which corresponds to the time of late September to late October; it is a pilgrimage festival, during which historically Jews travelled to the Temple in Jerusalem; it is celebrated to commemorate the ancient Israelites wandering for forty years in the desert after the exodus from Egypt

The first page of The Examination of the World by Rabbi Jedaiah ben Abraham Bedersi, from 1883, the book belonging to Chanoch Yoseph Borensztajn, Izyk Mendel's father, signed by the owner

I was speechless. I held the book tight to my heart, trying to grasp what had just happened. It seemed highly impossible the book of my dear father would find its way from Szczekociny to Israel, by some mysterious way reaching the son of the owner, the only survivor from the family. Another portion of excitement came when it turned out that the signature of my son Yossi (Yoseph), who was named after my father, bears a striking similarity to that of his grandfather, which he was never given to meet. The book reached us when Yossi's handwriting had already been formed, and he was a teenager. The way they write their name is precisely the same, both my father's signature and my son's. When I was moving to the United States, I decided to leave the invaluable gift at Yossi's house in Israel. I became deeply convinced that it belonged there.

Now I realize I cannot quell my hopes of trying to find a picture of my family. How much it would mean for me to see their faces again! Obviously, we did not have many photographs. Those days it was not that popular or possible, due to the fact of still developing slow technology. I do not dream about much, for even one would suffice. I think of the place my father had showed me when we were about to leave Szczekociny. After so many years, is there a sense at all to look for it?

I don't know how long I stand, looking bewildered at my family house, lost in thoughts. After a while, I decide to enter the neighboring yard of my childhood friend Kazimiera. We have been told by locals she still lives there. We pass through the gate, and I feel nothing changed here, there are the same old buildings at the back and yes, the same old apple trees! I look around and show my children where we used to play as children, how we would pick the fruits falling from the branches and eat them with pleasure. Such a beautiful and peaceful life did we use to have here!

Suddenly, I see an elderly woman coming out of the house and looking at us all; she seems a little confused about what is going on. For some period of time, she cannot actually understand the explanations of our guide Tomasz about who I am. Finally, she realizes. "Borensztajn!" she says. With extreme surprise, and great disbelief, she starts to realize I am the son of her neighbors; I am this boy who used to play with her and sit in the same bench at school. Her memory comes back, and I feel like I have come back from the beyond. She becomes extremely excited and cannot believe what is happening. She invites us to sit down and rest. She is truly warm and hospitable. At the same time, she cannot hide her emotions. We both rush to remind each other what it used to be like here and how we used to live. We sing the songs of our childhood in Polish, and I am surprised I remember them so well.

After a while I decide and ask her, "Do you think we could possibly see my house and enter inside?" "I will go and ask them," she replies. "Please wait here." My whole family is unanimously delighted at Kazimiera's personality. She comes back after a few minutes and leads us through the back door.

I am there, inside my dear house, back again. I am overwhelmed with numerous emotions, a peculiar mixture of happiness and suffering. It does not resemble my old good place, however. We enter the basement, which according to all logic, could still be the original place. It looks quite similar, but I cannot be sure. Most probably, the house was completely rebuilt, and this basement was built on the top of the old one. I feel truly disappointed. The house owner accompanies us and I don't feel comfortable in his company; neither do I feel courageous enough to ask him about anything. We leave.

Kazimiera's son, Krzysztof, brings a kind of comfort after this disappointing experience. It turns out he works in the municipality as the deputy of the town's mayor. He schedules our meeting in the archive and promises his help with retrieving any documents we need. In the meantime, we decide to continue the town's visit. I want to see the synagogue and the cemeteries, but before, we head for the school I used to attend. The building is still there, it is being renovated now, but I easily recognize it. We enter inside.

We used to learn in *Cheder* in the mornings and later, when we were six years old, in the afternoon we rushed to a public school. From the second grade on, it was the opposite. We started elementary school in the morning and we continued with our religious teacher in the afternoon. In my childhood times, school was six days a week; therefore we were obliged to attend classes on Saturdays, too. Since it is our holy day, *Shabbat*, and Jewish religious children could not fulfill this requirement, authorities facilitated it for us. To avoid any differences in teaching and thus our knowledge, children would study then practical skills and gymnastics, and we did not have to come to school on Saturdays. In the state school, we also had wonderful teachers, so patient and gentle. We liked them very much. I remember the name of my first teacher in that school, Ms. Mlekowna. We used to learn sitting in benches with tables, each of these for two children. From the very beginning I was sitting with my neighbor, Kazimiera. Each table had a hole with ink. Our pencil cases differed as for their content from what children take to school these days. Apart from pencils, rulers and compasses, we had feathers. We dipped them in the ink and this is how we used to write at that time.

Inside the school, during classes, we sat together, with no separation, on benches, Jewish and Catholics alike, and we respected one another without discrimination. I must admit most of Jewish children led in numerous subjects. We did not lead to any jealousy, however; we all were friends and, therefore, eagerly helped one another. Many times we were invited to their houses to do homework together.

I liked most subjects, but I particularly favored gymnastics and singing. I always liked sports. We often played volleyball, divided into two teams. The ball was big, so it was a challenge to win. I was very good at that, however, so both teams asked me to play with them. Also, I used to be very good at mathematics. I must admit I wasn't ashamed to tell teachers whenever they happened to make a mistake. Whenever other students had problems with understanding, the teacher would ask me to come to the board, and I always solved the task easily, explaining it at the same time to the rest of the class. I used to help my friend, the policeman's daughter, with mathematics, and she in turn helped me in geography, as it was her favorite subject.

I still remember the smell of the fresh bagels that our parents used to give us before we left for school. Even when we felt bad and didn't feel like going to school, the smell was so tempting that we could not resist it, so we simply took the bagel and decided to go. Only when our condition was really bad, did we resign and stay at home. I remember the smell of fresh potato latkes brought for us as lunch in winter. A woman came carrying a big pan and a knife to cut separate portions for each student, and it was still warm when we ate. She had a special agreement with our parents, who used to pay her every week. She also used to bring us special beans that were very big, white, and had a black spot. Unfortunately, I did not eat them again after I left Szczekociny. I could not find them anywhere.

If any teacher decided to pay a visit to a family during *Shabbat* or other holidays, it was considered the greatest honor for the whole family. Every parent tried hard to welcome them as best as they could. Younger children who did not study yet did not even dare to come out of their rooms when a teacher was visiting, such great respect was there for teachers.

I always liked to learn and tried to give as much as I could of myself. I didn't find it easy to attend both state and Hebrew school in two shifts, but, thank God, I managed somehow and was one of the best students in my class, with very good grades. I was always willing and eager to learn new things, no matter of the circumstances. I never thought I was too old for that.

In the 1980s, when we were moving to the United States with my family, I did not know English except for a few popular expressions. I was already fifty-seven years old at that time, but it was no obstacle for me. It took me few months only after the arrival to make myself completely understood. When I was over seventy, I learned to swim. If there is a will, there is a way; this always was my motto. I remember the sad verdict I heard from the doctors who found me in Gunskirchen, "We cannot save you." Against all the difficulties I had kept encountering on my way, I made it, and only a few years after the war I was in Israel; I was a soldier and a medic, a hard worker, a holder of a flat, and a husband of a religious woman I loved, starting my own family. There was a time such life was so fragile and improbable, I wouldn't even have dared to dream about it.

During my service for the Israeli Army, I had plenty of obligations. I was a commander responsible for the camps of Dura, Eliyahu and the units in Beit Lid. I could not complain about lack of responsibilities and duties. However, I was truly proud of the importance of my job and I tried to perform everything the best I could. Every day I issued orders with my signature. It was not an easy job, and I always kept all the recommendations and orders. Despite that, I decided to take a course in microbiology with other high school graduates. The gap between us was enormous. We came from extremely different environments, and with extremely different experiences. I lacked the calmness of their souls, which had never been disturbed with terror, panic, starvation, humiliation, and anguish, caused by the loss of family and home, deprivation of basic rights, and a total loss of control over body and mind as those of us who were survivors.

All of them spoke fluently Hebrew and English fluently, which discouraged me a little. I had been deprived of any chances to develop my education and had spent my best youth years working hard, imprisoned in Nazi camps. During that time, these young men who were now around me were investing in themselves, learning and developing.

When I became a soldier and when later I could no longer fight actively, I knew from the beginning what I would do instead. "I want to save people's lives," I answered when they asked me where I wanted to be moved. I wanted to help and cure people. I always had the longest queue of patients for injections or blood giving. "You don't feel anything when he does it," people said, recommending me to one another.

If only they knew where I had learned this! I was using the knowledge I had gained while working with Dr. Sperber in Auschwitz. All the appreciation and praise that came to me was thanks to the teacher I had. I couldn't stop thinking of the symbolism of this situation: a Jewish prisoner doctor teaching the basics of medicine in a concentration camp to another inmate miraculously saved from what seemed a certain death. After years, this helper, surviving even more traps on his way, would take advantage of this knowledge in the land where all Jewish history started. Back in Auschwitz, I had inserted needles into the skinny bodies of emaciated, terrified figures who were sentenced to death because they were Jewish. Here, I was helping strong, young men who created the Jewish Army and were protecting their Jewish state, which was just being constructed. How unpredictable Fate is! Time would prove that these were not the last circumstances in which I was to use this knowledge.

I was truly content knowing the appreciation of my patients. It also gave me some level of self-confidence. However, facing the professional exam during my soldier service, I felt insecure in the company of those who I considered better prepared. A voice inside me constantly filled me with doubts and disbelief. Yes, I did feel worse. I imagined them living their calm lives, coming back home to their parents, who gave them proper conditions for their educational development. I lacked this all; I was completely alone. Nobody was there to help me or support me; nobody was there to give me confidence and to believe in me. I hadn't had to study in a long time, and certainly my knowledge was of no comparison to other students. I still had a long way to overcome my lingering inferiority complexes.

Yet, filled with fears and doubts as I was, I also felt determined. In fact, I was motivated to work harder. I studied day and night alone. I listened carefully to each word the doctor said during his lectures. I tried to overcome the fear of failure that was lurking deep inside me. Eventually, to my deep astonishment, I received a diploma with only A and B grades! It was so touching for me. I sat looking at it overwhelmed with a mixture of emotions. I laughed happily that I had made it, even without knowing the languages or having high school background. Tears flowed down my face. I couldn't help the feeling of regret that I had no one to share this happiness with. There were no parents of mine waiting for me at home, to whom I would be able to proudly show my results. Yet, I must admit the good news gave me a boost of energy and added to my self-confidence. Soon after that, I decided to take driving lessons. Since the driving instructor used to give me the lessons in an ambulance, I became a qualified "ambulance driver," which was noted on my driver's license. From that point on, I transported ill soldiers whenever the ambulance driver was unwell himself.

I did not finish my education on these two improvements; it came only the first step. The success I achieved filled me with enough confidence to go up the ladder. Actually, I made an effort to go as far as I could within my profession, taking all possible courses and classes until I reached the top level. My self-esteem grew along with my salary and position. I appointed to more and more roles and had more responsibilities. I attended medical committees and filled out numerous documents of soldiers' conditions. With time, I became authorized to examine patients and choose a suitable treatment for them whenever doctors could not come themselves. There was never any complaint about my performance and I generally was treated with much respect and trust. The steps I had to take on my way provided very important lessons for me: the lesson of courage, persistence and self-confidence. My spirit got much better, and though apparently nothing had changed - I was still alone carrying my heavy past - I felt like I had been injected with another boost of energy, making me feel more and more stable in this new country, Israel.

My first school in Szczekociny will forever have a special place in my heart. We head towards the religious sites now, the synagogue, *Mykve* and cemeteries. Everything is very close in this small town, so very easily and quickly we reach the right place. However, I do not see the synagogue. In front of me, there is a building under construction, surrounded with a fence, with no roof. It looks like a warehouse. Probably the synagogue was bombed and destroyed during the war, and they built new houses here, I think. In the meantime, some locals gather around us. The news of our visit spreads quickly around the town. They claim that this is the old synagogue. I look at them, then at this building, and I say deeply convinced, "This is not the synagogue." I remember it used to have round windows, whereas in the building here they are rectangular. The locals keep assuring us it is. "It used to be a grain storehouse in the 1980s. Now there is a private owner," they say. This new information shocks me. I break down and cover my face with my hands. How can this be? It was such a magnificent synagogue.

It was once one of the most beautiful synagogues in Poland, quite big as for such a small town, and renowned all over the country. Inside, there was a Holy Ark with the ornaments and two cherubim and golden trumpets around; it was so high there were quite a few steps leading to it. There was our holy Scroll of *Torah*. The floor was marble, the curtain bright, shiny, and velvety. The Ten Commandments were written in gold letters. On the walls, there was a huge image of a leviathan and a buffalo. For a boy of eleven or twelve years old, as I was at that time, the images were so realistic that it seemed the animals were alive. I dreaded at the thought of staying there alone. However, looking at this image, my friends and I understood that indeed when Messiah comes, there would be enough portions for everyone during the feast with Leviathan's meat that our religion promises for the coming of Messiah. There was another drawing, which presented the tree of Adam and Eve. The ceiling resembled the sky, with its colors and images of clouds, stars, and the sun. It was a truly extraordinary work of art, difficult for me to describe.

The Synagogue in Szczekociny before the Second World War

The Bima and the Holy Ark inside the synagogue in Szczekociny, before the Second World War

The Holy Ark inside the synagogue in Szczekociny before the Second World War. The cover is a gift from Tadeusz Kosciuszko in gratitude for the support of Jews from Szczekociny in his battles

The arches inside the synagogue in Szczekociny before the Second World War

The synagogue building in Szczekociny 2004

The women's entrance was at least forty-to-fifty-feet tall, so that each one coming to pray could see and hear the cantor praying or reading *Torah*. There was a separate entrance to it. Each woman had a stand for her prayer book. I remember as a child looking up, trying to discern my mother, and hard as I tried, I couldn't.

Coming close and inside the Synagogue one could feel it is a holy place. The size and the height of the building were truly tremendous, and together with the inside ornaments, the Synagogue impressed everybody. We prayed there during holidays, sometimes in the week and of course each *Shabbat*.There was an absolute silence inside. It would be a shame for anyone to lose even one minute of the beautiful voice of the cantor, Pinkas Trajman. During High Holidays, the services were yet more ceremonious and we felt a great pleasure listening to the holy melodies. I used to sing here during that important time. I was in the choir with a friend, Fishel Stibelman. I remember they always asked me to sing during *Yom Kippur* and Rosh Hashana.

Szczekociny had two local rabbis. Rabbi Berek Ginsberg, appointed in 1913, held ceremonies and speeches, and ruled in matters of *Kashrut* and Shulchan Aruch, which is our law, the basis for everyday practice. The other was Rabbi Tsubiner. He was an instructor in the matters of marriage and divorce, quarrels between men and their wives and among friends, financial matters, menstruation, *Mezuzahs* [1], *tefillin*, and others. He functioned as an attorney according to the Jewish law, deciding on the punishment for the guilty. He was a respectable and likeable man with a truly dignified appearance. It was nice to look at him. He had a fair, long beard with *Peyes*. He knew several versions of prayers and had a beautiful, clear voice, which made him a wonderful singer. I really appreciated the way he prayed and liked to listen to him.

Now I cannot believe this is the same building. How is it possible they turned a place of prayers into a storehouse? The people in the town are religious; they respect their own church, why didn't they protect our synagogue? It belongs to them as well. It is not only about God's worshipping, it is a

1   *Mezuzahs*, Hebrew, doorposts with the prayer Hear, oh Israel that each religious Jew is obliged to place on the right side of the entrance to their house and each room inside

historical building! The faces of my family betray the same shock. We decide to enter inside, and right after a moment, it turns out we are definitely not welcome there. The workers cast curses and order us to leave immediately. They shout at us, and we feel truly endangered. Yossi manages to take a few pictures before we leave in a hurry. It is still possible to recognize the place for the Holy Ark, though the renovating works inside are quite advanced. Shocked and saddened as I am, I still don't know the worst is still to come.

There used to be two cemeteries in the town: the old one located next to the synagogue, and the new one, much bigger, on Lelowska Street, around a kilometer away from the town's center. It was close to the watermill on Pilica River, which was used for producing power. It belonged to Koppel Koppelovitz, and this fact made him famous in the town. Standing next to the synagogue, I realize the cemetery must be somewhere here, though obviously there are no signs of any tombstones. We come closer to the space, and the truth hits me with full power: I am in the old cemetery, with no gravestones, no fence around, but instead a private house and public toilets built on top of it. For a moment, we are all shocked and shaken so deeply we don't know what to say. My mother's family was buried here. Hundreds of Jews who used to live in this town for many years were to find here their place of eternal rest. Now there are toilets built on their bodies? It is grotesque. The locals again confirm what we refuse to believe; in the 1980s, the authorities built the public toilets for travelers of the nearby bus station. The private house was erected in the beginning of the 1990s. "It belongs to a local businessman," someone says. I look at this all in all impressive building and cannot believe it. "I can tell you that when they were building this house, many bones were uncovered." Somebody else adds, as if answering the question that I was scared to ask, "They threw them away."

The public toilets built on the Jewish cemetery ground, Szczekociny 2004

If I weren't a witness to this myself, I think I would have trouble believing it. Why? Was there not any other place in the whole town to build public toilets but on top of the graveyards of dead people? There is free space outside the cemetery but none within its borders! And who would like to live on the graves of dead people? Who digs the remains of innocent, dead people and throws them away as if they are rubbish? How is it possible?

I feel devastated. I seem to have lost all the strength and positive energy I had gathered so far, especially after meeting Kazimiera. I want to see if anything remains of *Mykve*, which was right in the street behind the synagogue, but I cannot find the place. Again, some of the building development has changed and I don't recognize the right building. Only three years later, during one of his visits, Yossi manages to find the right place with the help of David Richt, a survivor and the chairman at that time of the Szczekociny Jewish Organization of Survivors. It seems a new building was built on top of our ritual bath. The owners were suspicious, however, and didn't want to let them in. "There is nothing here," they said. "The house was built on the old ruins."

Sad and feeble now, I get into the car. We decide to check the situation with the new cemetery. I have no hope left. It would be a miracle they would save this cemetery after what had been done to other religious sites. When we reach the place within a few minutes, it turns out I was right. On its ground I see a factory. There are no remains of any gravestone. What happened to all those blocks? It is impossible that thousands of cement tombstones disappeared from this town; is it possible they were destroyed as well?

I am shaking at the thought of what could possibly have happened here too with the remains of my family members. When I was eight years old, we buried here my dear grandmother, Esther Rachel. I was very close to her; she lived with us until her death. She was always there for me. Two years later, my dear sister, Hannah Fagel, passed away at the age of seventeen due to the erysipelas she developed. She had a serious problem with her leg, which did not heal, and she died so young. I remember when my parents took us here to show us where our grandfather and uncles were buried. We took care of their tombs and read the Book of Psalms for the transcendence of their souls to Heaven. I used to come here and pray; I participated in the funeral ceremonies of the towns' people and my father's friends. Now, their gravestones are razed to the ground, their bones devastated and removed from the place that was supposed to be their eternal rest.

The truth comes yet more difficult to accept when we later find out there is an old Christian cemetery in the town, quite well-preserved and taken care of. I know these were Germans who started the obliteration of our culture with all its traces, but to learn that Polish people, Christians, our neighbors, completed their plan is truly painful. I remember how we used to live in mutual friendship and tolerance before the war; what changed with time? What happened to those people? It becomes obvious to me they took our houses; they had nowhere to live after bombings and, apparently, there were no Jews in the town anymore. However, I cannot come to terms with the fact that they not only failed to take proper care of our holy, religious sites, but they devastated and desecrated them with no heart. I am speechless and need to rest. I don't know yet what to do, but I know I will not leave it like that. My children come with their full support. Yossi decides to act immediately. "We need to see the mayor," he says decisively.

"It's terrible what they did to these cemeteries," we suddenly hear behind us. "You should make a complaint at the mayor's." We look around and see a local lady, whose words come as confirmation and acceptance of our next steps. "I remember when they dug all the bones from here and left them in the corner, over there." She points to one of the directions. "The skulls were lying there for a long time, many people saw them." Probably later they were thrown away, just like with the old cemetery. With time, she reveals that even her young son used to come and play with skulls there, which seems completely incomprehensible to me.

During the conversation, it turns out the land of the new cemetery belongs to the same owner. For the second time this day, we hear his ominous name. He bought these two cemeteries and built his glass and concrete manufacturing factory on top of the new one, and his private house on the ground of the old one, next to the public toilets. We are told that it used to stand a slaughterhouse here before. We feel extremely dismayed and upset.

The lady invites us to try and talk to her ninety-year-old father, who remembers a lot from before and after the war, as she assures us. When we reach the place, the old and feeble man gets uncertain, and first of all points at Yossi, asking, "Is he from the police?" He doesn't calm down, and there is no sense making him even more nervous. We leave slightly disappointed.

The woman tells us however, that there are still tombstones in the town, and gives us information on where we can find them. "Most of them were used as bricks for rebuilding destroyed houses," she explains. "You can still find some serving as pavement here and there. I will show you." On the place, a man shows us a well-preserved gravestone. We look at it, equally touched, the only Jewish artifact we manage to see in the town, which used to be peopled for hundreds of years by thousands of Jews. The man agrees to give us the tombstone. While walking away, my son, Yossi, suddenly stops and looks bewildered at one of the pavement tiles. I come closer. We have found another gravestone, which now serves as a walking facility. The man agrees we dig it out, and here we have a proof. Apart from the shape of an oval Jewish matzeva, there are also Hebrew letters at the back side. We look around and discover more of them! Eventually, we dismantle a section of the pavement, which proves to be built of Jewish tombstones. We leave with these few precious stones, which happen to be the only remains of this town, once vibrant with Jewish culture. Yossi and Zvika carry them carefully to our van. The first idea is to take them to Warsaw, to our guide's house and later to organize a way to take them to Israel, to prevent them from further desecration.

While loading them inside, we are visited by another local, a young lady. "When you finish here," she says, "please come to my place there. I have some more." We reach her yard after a few minutes, and inside it we are stunned at the sight. There, we see the whole pile of gravestones! "I have been waiting years to give them back to the Jews," she explains. We are amazed at the amount. Though the vast majority of them are broken into smaller pieces, one can still see clearly what they are and what purpose they used to serve. I stand there, bewildered as I look at this amazing view, and finally reach out to take one. I hold this precious item carefully and try to read the letters with tears in my eyes. To my amazement, it says, "Crying," and it shows also eyes with tears. Now I know why I have come back here and why it could happen only now, sixty years after. I feel the tears of Szczekociny Jews running into my eyes. I feel the restlessness of their souls. Their crying has brought me here to speak for them, and tell the world that all Szczekociny Jews have been murdered; some perished during the Holocaust, others were eradicated from the remembering by those who survived and came after the war.

Izyk Mendel Bornstein during his first visit after the war in Szczekociny, 2004. The piece of the gravestone that he is holding says in Hebrew, crying

We decide to change our decision; obviously we cannot take them all with us. The woman, Ewa, agrees to take more from other yards, and care for them. Slowly a bigger plan is born in our minds. There must be something done, something to prevent any further desecration of any religious objects, and at the same time, something to commemorate the memory of the towns' Jewish population. It comes as an internal must.

First of all, however, we feel an urge to see the town's authorities. The mayor, Wieslaw Grycner, is first of all surprised with the field of our interest. "I have had many guests from Israel, survivors and their descendants," he says. "They wanted to regain their property. You had such a nice house," he turns to me, "and you keep talking only about the cemeteries and the synagogue."

"I have a place to live," I answer him, "but I cannot leave these things. It is incomprehensible and shocking to destroy religious objects, which belong to our common past." I say. "As the head of this town, you are responsible for the right order here, and, therefore, we ask you to take this decision and pull the toilets down."

The mayor does not know what to answer for a moment. He seems confused. He blames the previous communist regime for such decision. "The toilets are used by citizens and the house belongs to a private person. I cannot do anything. You'd better go back home, and leave it as it is. I cannot help you."

My son interrupts him, "Do you think it could happen, if it were a Christian cemetery?" The mayor holds his tongue and spreads his hands helplessly. "How would you feel," Yossi asks then, "if they built public toilets on top of your parents' graves?"

Though dramatic, this question does not seem to bring any change. The mayor keeps repeating that he cannot do anything, and we get more and more depressed. It seems we will achieve nothing. "There were Jews coming here before you. They complained about the toilets, but then they left and never came back," the Mayor sighs, suggesting it will be the same with us.

I know, however, that I will not be able to sleep calmly until the toilets disappear from the cemetery place. Finally, we feel we have no other choice but to warn him. "We do not want any fights, but if you leave us no other choice, we will have to act differently, through different organizations and media." We leave feeling deeply saddened and disregarded. Was what we asked for really something difficult to understand? To stop pouring excrement on the land where there still are some remains of human bodies. Did it make a difference what bodies they were? Did one's religion make a difference in such a case?

I am completely astounded by what I found here: appalling acts done to the holy remains of my ancestors, to the whole Jewish community of the town. The truth of contemporary Szczekociny is painful, but I do not regret for a second coming back here. On the contrary, I realize now what this shy inner voice encouraging me to come here could be. Slowly, I realize my mission in reaching this town again. I keep thinking of the future and what must be done. I know I will not rest until this wrong is made right again. My family will help and support me during the process. I am not alone. I leave the town with important declarations and plans in my heart. We head for Wodzislaw, my father's hometown, where I last saw my parents and sisters.

ELEVEN

We came to Wodzislaw in January 1940: my parents, my two younger sisters and my brother Jacob. Schlomo was already living in Kielce at that time with his wife; so was my older sister Sara and her husband. Hannah Fagel had already been dead for a few years at that time. On the place we found a well-organized ghetto with centralized Jewish life there. We entered these conditions, accepting slowly the difficult fact that we were to live in war times with no guarantees. Each day would be an attempt to survive. No more could we simply go to a shop and buy anything we wanted. Germans controlled everything, and shops were mainly empty, containing only necessary products in limited quantities. We all got special cards allowing us to buy only certain amounts of basic products. The needs were estimated by the number of people in the family, and what we got was bread and milk; at times we managed to find other dairy. We were happy we had anything to eat at all. True hunger changes the attitude to food. We used to go to a bakery and stand there until late at night to get some bread. I remember long queues of tired people. "God, please, make there be enough for me," we prayed hoping not to face empty shelves when our turn came. Hard times though these were, we always tried to share whatever we had with other people.

Obviously, we were not allowed to leave the specified area. Anything we did, anywhere we moved, it was within the borders of the ghetto. We were trapped as animals, permanently watched and punished for disobedience. Where could we go? It was mainly the question of getting food or attending prayers, which gave us some hope and strength to go on. Nazis slowly tightened the restrictions.

One day my father brought sad news home. "They want our valuables. We have two weeks." We couldn't believe it. All the Jewish community had to gather gold, jewelry, and any other valuable objects we possessed and transfer it to the German commission. After that period of time, a revision was planned. "You know the punishment, should we find anything," they said.

This made my mother completely break down. She had some gold saved for hard times, and she had hoped she would be able to use it later. It had given her a feeling of security that she would lose now. It was not only the hard-earned and saved coins. Though it provides safety, money is nothing in situations where life is at stake. What must have bothered her more were the priceless wedding gifts that Nazis reached for with their greedy, insatiable hands: silverware that my parents used during *Shabbat* and holidays, the *Kiddush* [1] cup that my father, through all these years, used for blessing wine, candlesticks that my mother cherished whenever she was blessing the light. They were more than just objects; they were part of our religious, sacred life. Now we had to give them away. My father, like others in all Jewish families, put them all in a strong canvass bag and, without asking unnecessary questions, silently took them to a specified place.

At that time we did not understand yet that this process was something more than to deprive us of valuables and destroy our confidence. It was a mission aimed at obliteration of our entire culture, with all signs of its traditions and customs. At that moment, we had not a bigger perspective; it was still the beginning. We hoped that soon things would get back to normal. People recalled the First World War. They did not know yet that these Germans, though from the same country that gave birth to the highest culture and art, were far beyond any comparison to those who came years ago. Soon we all were to experience it ourselves.

In the meantime, people obediently brought the valuables of their lives, giving away their savings built up for entirely different purposes, apprehensive about cherished *Chanukah* and *Menorah* [2] candlesticks and other religious utensils they had to put now in front of their tormentors. Women were taking off their precious jewelry given by their husbands and parents, often with all family stories passed from generation to generation. Nobody protested. Life had the highest value for us all. Yet, deep inside, our hearts were crying bitter tears at this cruel injustice.

---

1 *Kiddush*, Hebrew, literally "sanctification", a blessing recited over the wine or grape juice to sanctify *Shabbat* or Jewish holiday

2 *Menorah*, Hebrew, a seven branched candlestick; a symbol of Judaism for almost three thousand years, the emblem of Israel, one of the oldest symbols of Jewish people which stood in the Temple

We lived that limited freedom, encountering more and more constraints, until 1942. It was more difficult for us, my brother, Jacob Hersh, and my two sisters Rivka Zysla and Ita Golda, since we did not know anybody there or the town itself. We missed our good Szczekociny, our home there, and our calm life before the invasion. We kept wondering what was happening there, how our neighbors and friends were dealing with these difficulties. Were they suffering more than us here? What became of our house? Were there Germans living there now, using our rooms, our belongings? Would we be able to come back there? My father, who was born and raised in Wodzislaw, found it quite easier; apart from that he was the head of the family, and he felt obliged to take care of us all. Yet, it must have been difficult for him too, to see his hometown changed into a prison for his community, who, like in other Polish cities and towns, had to be secluded from the rest of the town and its people, as the most dangerous enemy of the invaders. It was very difficult to understand. What wrong had we done living our quiet life in Szczekociny, as all the others, to be punished like this and treated as the worst of humankind?

In the autumn of 1942, before the time of High Holidays, my father made that difficult decision to send Jacob and me away in order to save our lives. It was the last time I was in this town. After what I saw in Lelov and Szczekociny, I feel completely disillusioned and do not expect much. I only want to again view the town from where my father's family came, where we spent our last moments together before the worst came.

We enter the city and stop at the synagogue. Inside, our eyes meet a sad scene. Wild plants, trees, and weeds overgrow the place. Some of the walls look as if they are going to collapse. I remember when we used to come and pray here during those two ghetto years. The war, the ghetto, the fear, and slow deprivation did not, on the whole, restrain people from continuing a religious life. On the contrary, many turned to God more often, some with trust, some with fear, some with anger - people wanted to understand why they were tried so severely and when that would come an end. This place, the remains of the synagogue, is painful for me not only due to its condition. It is the place of one of the greatest tragedies within my family.

A few years after the war, when I was already married and living in Israel, I was participating within the meetings of the Szczekociny Jewish Organization, a group of survivors from my hometown that used to gather once a year for a memorial day, praying for Szczekociny Jews at the monument raised to their memory in Holon[1]. During one such meeting in the 1950s, I started a conversation with one of the survivors who also happened to be in the ghetto in Wodzislaw. He decided he should tell me a very painful piece of information he knew.

On *Yom Kippur* of September 21, 1942, not long after I had left with Jacob, during the ceremonies in the synagogue, my father, a Rabbi, was carrying the scroll of the *Torah* during the service of *Kol Nidrei*[2], when suddenly a few Nazis entered brutally inside, screaming and profaning the prayers.

"They went right to your father," he told me the details, while I felt my heart contorting with pain, "and killed him with a quick, cold shot to his head. They took him by his beard then and yelled to the crowd *"Wo ist dein Gott jetzt?"*[3].

I feel my world fall apart again. I need to be strong, I told myself, I wanted to listen to the end.

"Then, they fired some careless bullets into the crowd," he continued. "They did not bother to execute everybody, the transport to Treblinka had already been well-planned at that time."

Though overwhelmed with pain and suffering, I needed to know more details: "What happened later? What did they do to his body?" I asked thrilled, "Where are his remains now?" His words pierced me through: "Don't ask please about anything more. It is better for you not to know anything else."

---

1   Holon, a city in Israel in the district of Tel Aviv. On its cemetery, a monument devoted to the Jewish Community of Szczekociny was built within the first years after the Second World War. It was initiated and sponsored by Abraham Schwartzbaum, a survivor from Szczekociny and the first chairman of Szczekociny Jewish Organization

2   *Kol Nidrei*, Arameic, a Jewish prayer recited in the synagogue at the beginning of the evening service on *Yom Kippur*, its name is taken from the opening words, meaning "All vows", refers also to the whole *Yom Kippur* evening service

3   *Wo ist dein Gott jetzt*, German, Where is your God now?

Shocked and petrified I followed his advice. The truth might have crushed me completely. Maybe it was better not to know? However, still a long time after this event I cannot stop thinking about what I was told as well as of what I was advised not to ask. My dear father, whom I tried to protect so long by walking to work instead of him because of that precise reason, his beard. I dreaded that his beard, which made him stand out as being Jewish, would tempt some oppressors to violence.

Izyk Mendel Bornstein supported by his children at the remains of the Wodzislaw synagogue's Holy Ark, the place where his father was murdered by the Nazi during the Second World War. Wodzislaw, 2008

Here and there the stories of persecutions reached us and saddened deeply. My dear father, so righteous until the end. Even though he realized obvious risk, he did not resign from performing religious observances during our holiest day. I could not stop shaking, though I was grateful to my informer for sharing this difficult information with me. My mind kept producing the images of this horrible event. I kept asking myself what they did later with him. What happened to my mother and sisters? Did the truth manage to reach them before, as I presume, they were loaded onto the cattle tracks and taken to Treblinka? Painful questions and no answers, but I tried to accept not having them. I knew the knowledge would probably bring even more suffering.

The moment Jacob and I said goodbye to our parents and sisters in Wodzislaw was the last time I saw them. The letter from my dear brother was the last sign I had from him, upon which I could also deduce what had happened to him and my uncle. I may suspect my mother with my sisters were loaded onto cattle-trucks, and together with the rest of the approximately three thousand Jews from Wodzislaw, they were brutally murdered and exterminated in Treblinka. Their deportation, which I found out years after, coincided with the liquidation of the ghetto in Szczekociny, whose Jewish population was treated in the same, well-planned way[1].

Yom Kippur, though believed to be a special and most important day for each Jew, has come to mean much more in my life. It was the period of *Yom Kippur* that the Jewish communities of Szczekociny and Wodzislaw, the towns of my families, were destroyed and taken for extermination. It was *Yom Kippur* that my dear father lost his life in such a meaningful way, during the time that his friends, family, and neighbors from Szczekociny were marched to the nearest railway station and taken to Treblinka, crowded into cattle trucks. It was also *Yom Kippur*, when I was sentenced for death, shot at and then dressed in white clothes, saved for the remaining long years of my life. During my service in the synagogue in Harrisburg, in United States, I would always ask to hold the scroll of *Torah* during *Kol Nidrei* praying. In this way, I united with my dear father and symbolically finished the service for him.

My yearning for my dear family has never been satiated. Right after the war, I did not stop my vigilance for any news about them. A flick of hope that survived with me through all the atrocities was possibly being reunited

---

1   According to available historic resources, the transports of Jews from Szczekociny (1,500) and Wodzislaw (3,000) took place from the 16th to the 25th September 1942. Szczekociny survivors recall it was the eve of *Yom Kippur* of 1942, which allows for more precise date specification, i.e. September 20, 1942

with my family. If I survived the war, thanks to so many incomprehensible turns of fate, perhaps somebody else from the rest of my family also did? It is only time that made me get used to the situation that I was alone and I should not expect it would be changed. Deep inside, I have never come to terms with that fact. All my life, regardless of my deep gratitude for everything I have achieved and received, I have felt lonely.

Since I was released from the hospital in Austria, when my bones were covered with a decent level of skin, thanks to the treatment I received there and contrary to the gloomy prediction made by the camp doctors, I was slowly learning how to be a human again, not a number. Mendel Borensztajn was born again. I got used to the fact that I had a name. I was washed with the pleasure of calm voices around me, which spoke without hatred or threats. What was obvious and natural for others, I had to bring back to my life, cautiously, carefully, making sure it was true, that it was real and it would not crash down on me like in all those dreams from which I had to awake. I had to get used to living without fear and without the habitual need for vigilance. I had to learn again to trust people around me, not to see potential killers in them, not to be afraid of being hit or humiliated. At the same time, I was in the process of learning to cope alone in the new world, to depend on myself, and accept the fact that at least I managed to survive, and can start a family to continue what my ancestors started.

Then, in 1945, I thought about Szczekociny. Our house had probably been lost forever, but I wondered where I could go to find my family, if they had survived the war too. Most of the Jewish survivors, me included, were located in various transit camps. I was placed in Munich; there we all could decide upon our further destination. I remembered my father's wish to leave for Palestine, when the war had been about to come. I felt this would be the most probable goal of my family. Just like many other survivors, I decided myself that I would head there. Hardly anyone wanted to go back to Poland, where we had experienced the worst and where probably nothing was left of our properties. The soldiers explained to us they would take us to Italy and from there to Palestine. We had to be prepared for that process. Though it seemed the only place in the world we Jews could claim, though we were deprived of homes in Europe, Palestine was under the British mandate, and the number of newcomers was strictly controlled. We would have to come illegally. At that time, however, while we were still recovering slowly, we did not find this fact particularly bothersome.

This is how I came to Italy. In the summer of 1945, I arrived in the city of Modena, from where I was transferred to Nonantola, together with other survivors. Here, they built a *Kibbutz* for us, which we called Nonantola *Kibbutz*. We did not know each other, but we were all Jewish survivors, so we tried hard to get closer to one another and to share our experiences. We remained under the supervision of a Jewish brigade of the British army, and we followed their orders. They treated us really well, trying to make up for all we had suffered before to give us the taste of positive emotions and remind us what the world could be. They had an entertainment program for us. Everything was carefully planned. Almost every day, they took us out. We enjoyed movies, concerts, theater shows, singing, and dancing - simply spending a good time with our comrades. The inside of the Italian cinemas and theaters was truly beautiful. I took enormous pleasure just to look at the decorations and design. I had never seen such a thing before. At one time we were even taken for sightseeing in different regions of Italy. After approximately the-half year we spent there, I was able to speak basic Italian. I could go and do the shopping alone, and I learned a few Italian songs; some of them I still remember. After what we had seen and experienced during the last years, we were slowly learned how to live freely and we enjoyed the beauty of the world to which we came back. Everything seemed so new, colorful, beautiful and modern.

Jewish Refugees in Italy.
- 13 -

BOJARSKI	Gitel	Debretzin	(Ung.)	1922	Jakob	Sara
"	Shmuel	Sluack	(Pol.)	1914	Jehuda	Chana
BOJM	Zehawa	Kowel	"	1921	Moshe	Chaja
BOK	Meir	Poland		1919	Leibish	Rachel
BOKOW	Noach	Ruble-Polese		1904	Dawid	Pessa
BOKSENBAUM	Moshe	Ozarow	(Pol.)	1925	Jehuda	Chawa
BOKSER	Joachim	Drohobicz	"	1928	Dawid	Fanja
"	Tola	"	"	1924	"	"
BOLDO	Meshulem	Poland		1890	Shmuel	Rachel
"	Pesia	"		1892	Zwi	"
BOLESLAWSKI	Dawid	"		1906	Fishel	Manja
BOMBALSKI	Usher	Grujec	(Pol.)	1923	Manes	Chaja
BOMOWICZ	Israel	Warszawa	"	1901	Eliezer	Chjena
BONGEROW	Moshe	Lodz	"	1922	Shulim	Rachel
BORECKA	Chana	Zawjeroze	"	1920	Tooch	Elte
BORGER	Emiel	Poland		1892	Herman	Anna
"	Stelja	Austria		1900	Maks	Olga
BORISOW	Imanuel	Odesa	(Rus.)	1928	Jakob	Pola
BORKOWITS	Dow	Mako	(Ung.)	1927	Israel	Chana
BORNSTEIN	Abraham	Lodz	(Pol.)	1917	Fishel	Pessia
"	"	Radom	"	1929	Israel	Rachel
"	Alfred	Bjelsko	"	1902	Josef	Eta
"	Beniek	Lodz	"	1928	Abraham	Zelde
"	Fela	-		1920	Icohak	Reizel
"	Hinda	Wjolun	(Pol.)	1920	Jakob	Perla
"	Hirsh	Sorooa	(Rus.)	1910	"-David	Chaja
"	Leon	Shkud	(Lit.)	1914	Tobia	Jenia
"	Mejer	Wizorez	(Pol.)	1922	Leib	Ester
"	Mendel	Poland		1914	Simche	Freide
"	"	Szczekocin	"	1927	Josef	Lea
"	Moshek	Warszawa	"	1926	Shloma	Fejga
"	Pinchas	Zechlin	"	1918	Abraham	Ester
BORER	Mendel	Radom	"	1936	Welwel	Toiba
BOROWIK	Ebi	Bjalistok	"	1925	Shmuel	Chana
BOROWSKI	Dawid	Poland		1910	Moshe	Hana-Batja
BOROWSKA	Ester	Warszawa	"	1914	Alter	Chana
BORUCHOWICZ	Salomon	Lithuania		1912	Elchanan	Werka
BORUCHSON	Nechama	Kowno	(Pol.)	1926	Icohak	Feiga
BORSUK	Abram	Poland		1911	Moshe	Shoshana
BORZYNOWSKY	Benjamin	Czenstochow	"	1916	Jechiel	Lea
BOSKOWITZ	Berta	Yugosl.		1873	Moritz	Rosa
BOTSHAN	Hershel	Bjalistok	(Pol.)	1912	Asher	Mirjam
BOTWINIK	Dow	Wilna	"	1920	Gershon	Manja
"	Salda	"	"	1923	Dow	Mussaia
BOZNIAK	Hackiel	Lodz	"	1906	Moshe	Mirjam
BRAFMAN	Mordchaj	Chrzanow	"	1923	Josef	Lea
"	Moric	Poland	"	1928	Shloma	Mirl
BRAININ	Berta	Katowice	"	1917	Leib	Zila
BRAITER	Josef	Krakow	"	1923	Jeshijahu	Sara
BRAMSTEIN	Chaja	C.S.R.	"	1926	Herman	Perl
"	Icohak	"	"	1927	"	"

A copy of a list of Jewish Refugees in Italy. This list was created in the immediate postwar era. Mendel Bornstein's name appears near the middle of this page. This list provides Mendel Borstein's name, date of birth, place of birth, nationality, and parents' first names

What we all had to learn first of all, however, was our attitude toward food. For a long time I couldn't get used to the feeling of satiation in my stomach. Everything was so tasty and nourishing. I discovered tastes anew after long years of starvation. We were provided with three substantial meals a day, and since it was Italy, quite often we were served pasta. After six years of being fed watery soups and tough bread, each type of real food tasted like heaven for us all, and each meal surprised us with its amount. Some of us ate greedily, as if still fearful it could be taken or stolen; others, on the other hand, cherished each bite, celebrating the dream that had come true. Slowly we were getting used to the freedom that was granted us, and we started to feel new life coming.

I will never forget the excitement that arose inside me one day, when they announced on the speakers that someone was looking for Mendel Bornstein. It was difficult to believe it at first. I was very cautious and tried to calm myself. Was it really me? Was it my name? It must have meant that somebody from my family survived and was looking for me! Maybe Jacob? Maybe one of my sisters? I flew to the meeting with my heart beating fast, full of both apprehension and high hopes. When I arrived at the place, however, I found my old friend from Szczekociny, Faibel Traiman, wearing a British Brigade uniform. Slowly, my excitement went away, and I was filled with disappointment. Of course, it was good to see a well-known face from my hometown, from those safe times before the war. But, the loss of the warm promise of meeting even one of my family members, left me disappointed again.

Faibel was very happy to see me. He kissed me and hugged me tightly, smiling radiantly. He took me out to a restaurant, where he bought me some chocolate bars. We spent a few hours there, talking and sharing our experiences, crying and recollecting the past that had gone forever. He gave me the address of Shoshana Kirshentsweig, our friend from Szczekociny. As most of us, she was the only survivor from her family and yet another alive from our small town. She was already in Israel.

Faibel had a good suggestion for me. "Contact her. Maybe she can help you. Maybe she has some news you would like to know."

All in all, even with all the disappointment at first, the meeting cheered me up a little. Obviously, nothing could heal my awakened expectations to see my dear family, but meeting an old friend in such lonely times was soothing as well. Years later, we met again in Israel, where he asked me to witness for him. He was about to get married, and he was in need of someone to sign his *Ketubah* [1] and certify he was a single man.

Faibel Traiman, a Holocaust survivor from Szczekociny, a friend of Izyk Mendel Bornstein

In the meantime, I continued the preparations for the plan of going to Palestine. Each day, the soldiers taught us how to walk on thick rope, and how to get into a ship without being caught. Most of them had guns, and they also taught us how to use them; of course they used wooden bullets, not to kill anybody. I myself liked all these procedures and was quite good at them, and eventually I had a group. I taught them how to climb onto ships, how to walk on a rope and use guns, and how to put them up and down. Soon after we were taught how to dismantle and clean perfectly weapons, I became an instructor for *Haganah* [2], until we reached Palestine.

Since the British Brigade had limited the arrival of Jewish displaced persons,

---

1   *Ketubah*, Hebrew: a document, a written agreement reached before a wedding, where a man commits himself to provide food, clothing and marital relations to his wife, as well as to pay her a certain amount of money in case of divorce

2   *Haganah*, Hebrew The defense, a Jewish paramilitary organization during the existence of British Mandate for Palestine, from 1920 to 1948, created to protect Jewish *Kibbutzim* during Arab riots

we were being trained how to enter the place without being detected. We were to be illegal cargo on a ship, which would apparently be carrying chickens. I was so impatient to reach the shores and start my new life there, in the Holy Land! No obstacle could discourage me.

Finally, our long expected happy moment arrived. We were going to our Promised Land. We all were so excited! They took us to Port Genoa in Italy, where the ship Anchi Sireni was waiting for us. The Brigade received a certificate from the British to transfer 1,200 chickens, which were to come on this ship. We, over a thousand people, would be a hidden, as additional transport. Around 40 percent of us were Russian Partisans. Trained and skillful, they knew how to use weapons and what to do in case the British officers caught us. In the dark we boarded the ship and took our place there. It was so crowded inside that we lay on canvas hammocks tied high three in a row; whenever the one on the top hammock needed to go out, mostly because of nausea, the other two below had to make space for him getting up too. Most of the people had problems with that kind of travel. I myself felt very good.

After a day or two, we reached a shore, and they told us to get off the ship. What happened? The journey was supposed to take over two weeks! We were truly surprised, and asked one another, "Are we in Israel already? Impossible!"

We disembarked the ship slowly and hesitantly to see the same place we had left not long ago. In our disappointment, we started to fear we would not be able to go. Soon, the circumstances were explained; the British the British were monitoring new arrivals closely and it was too dangerous to go. We would certainly have been caught. Our officers made a decision to play it safe until further notice and then try again. So we did. We waited impatiently in the camp and we hoped that our journey was only the question of time, that we would not be stopped again, and that nobody would take this dream from us. After a few days, the decision came: "All aboard!" We tried again. We were going to our new, awaited home. Fate, please do not disappoint us that time! We thought.

It did not. We kept sailing, and each day we got further from Italy, we prayed nobody would stop us again. Each day we were given very light food: hot, sweet semolina porridge in the morning, crackers and sardines for the rest of the day. Yet, many people had problems again with the ship swaying, going sick after every portion of porridge. I was lucky enough to endure the whole journey with no stomach problems. I thought about what it would be like in the new country. I knew I had made the right decision, yet, how could I manage with a new land, new language? My thoughts were also about what I was leaving behind. I was saying goodbye to the places that had shaped me since the beginning; Poland, Austria, Italy. My heart was overwhelmed with sorrow and nostalgia after my beloved hometown Szczekociny and everything I experienced there, my peaceful childhood among my dear family, happy and carefree days until all our dreams and expectations were brutally quenched. Within a mere six years, my life completely changed the direction it seemingly had been going. It went out of control, and I had to face the new reality that led me here, where I was standing, a completely different man. Who would have ever suspected in our past that at the age of twenty-one I would be separated from our entire family, a sole survivor of unimaginable war atrocities, on my way to Palestine?

It took us two-and-a-half weeks before we reached the shores of the Promised Land. Haifa! We all felt sheer elation. We started to sing from our hearts, *Hevenu Shalom Aleichem*[1]! Finally, after all this insecurity, we were here! However, though we had planned to avoid it, we got detained by the British Army. They ordered the partisans to throw all weapons into the sea, treated us with oranges, and they took us to the Athlit Camp. They were nice to us, and because we were all so happy to finally be in our expected destination, we did not feel that being detained again deprived us of our precious, eventually regained freedom. In a way, however, we were imprisoned again. Fortunately, the conditions were good, and we could feel safe. There were no tormentors lurking cannily around.

The British used to make sure all of us were in beds at 10:00 p.m. each night. However, it was difficult for some of us to fulfill this requirement. There were some among us who liked to stay longer in the town, watching movies or having fun. We obviously did not want them to face any problems; therefore,

---

1   *Hevenu Shalom Aleichem*, Hebrew, "we bring peace upon you" a popular Jewish song

we always tried hard to shape their beds with pillows and blankets so that these resembled human beings. Fortunately, the soldiers did not check things too carefully but simply counted the shapes in beds, which saved our joyful friends from punishment. We all had got close to one another during the time spent in Italy. We all considered each other good friends. The Jewish Agency provided us with decent food, and we sang during our meals. All in all, we were here. Our Holy Land stretched in front of us, and we all were impatient to set our feet on its ground! We had been informed we would have to spend two weeks in the camp, so we prepared a short calendar helping to count off the remaining days. Each day we crossed out the one that passed, and we were happy to see the time going. Our joy was great and true. We knew we would finally be let into the country; therefore, we kept our spirits high.

Finally, the great day came. We crossed out the last day on our calendar! We were visited by a few Jewish Agency people, who started to relocate us into several different *Kibbutzim*. They interviewed us and asked where we would like to go and what we intended to do there. I did not know anything about Palestine, except for what I had read in the Bible. I knew some names of the cities, most of all Tel Aviv, so I told them I would like to go there. Thus, I was sent to Tel Yizhak, near Even Yehuda, in the vicinity of Natanya. The person from the Jewish Agency comforted me, saying, "Listen, Mendel, don't worry at all. You are now in Israel, and in our *Kibbutz*. You will get everything you need. Here, we wear shorts, eat onion bread and are happy. You will become a member of the *Kibbutz*, so don't worry about the work. We will teach you the language too. Soon everything will come into its place." I felt quite reassured with what he told me. After what I left behind, nothing should worry or scare me anymore, I comforted myself.

I shared a tent with three other friends. I was assigned for work on banana plantations together with Meir Lublinsky, a *Kibbutz* member and a truly nice man. I worked really hard moving the sprinklers from place to place, to water the banana trees, trimming overgrowing plants, all in the burning heat of the summer. I was not used to such weather conditions. Summers in Poland were much milder! Fortunately enough, most of the people, who were also European survivors, spoke Yiddish, and I could make myself understood, not knowing Hebrew yet. Most of the people were very friendly, however,

I remember one event that was somewhat surprising to me. Once, during a *Kibbutz* meeting, when our everyday life issues were being discussed, I came up with a suggestion of improvement our daily life. I had an idea and wanted to share it, maybe it would be helpful?

One of the men from the board looked at me and said, "Listen, a dog before a year does not bark, all right?" I was surprised at this hostility, for I had good intentions, but I accepted the rule. It was made clear that they only allowed those who had already spent some time there to speak.

Despite all these small obstacles, we were all very happy. We were working as farmers in our holy land; we had our food, clothes, and laundry services provided and most of all, we were free men, no longer humiliated, intimidated, starved, and threatened, with death lurking on each step. Of course, we all carried our wounds, but we were going on, and the future seemed brighter each day. Helpful people around, a friendly atmosphere, sun and warmth, and the fact we were busy all day building our new lives. All these conditions were very helpful at dragging our pain away. I made good friends there, among them Elisha Rozani, Moshe Kreshniker, Yishaya Rabinovitz and David Rabinovitz. We used to spend a lot of time together after work, visiting the vicinity, talking, and enjoying our freedom in the new land.

To whom it may concern.

This is to certify that

Mr. *BORNSTEIN MENDEL*

has been RELEASED from Clearance Camp, Athlit

on *4. II 46*

The certificate confirming Izyk Mendel Bornstein's release from the Athlit clearance camp, Palestine, 1946

The inside of the Palestinian identity card of Izyk Mendel Bornstein, 1946

Soon after my arrival, I sent a letter to Shoshana Kirshentsweig, as we had decided with Faibel in Italy. After a few weeks, a reply came. She invited me to come and spend *Shabbat* with her and her husband in Ra'anana. It was a very nice surprise, which cheered me up. I would see another familiar face from my town, and maybe she could give me some information, I hoped. The only problem was how to get to Ra'anana. Let's try, I thought, going to the main road with the intention of stopping a car that would take me to my destination. I stood there, on Friday morning, watching British Army trucks passing by, one after another, and waving at each one to stop. My patience paid off, and after a short while I was climbing up and took my place at the back of the car. At Ra'anana, I did the same, and soon was knocking at Kirshentsweig's door. "It is a great honor for us," they said welcoming me warmly. "Thank you for accepting our invitation." They were truly happy to have me as their guest, and I felt moved at this meeting too.

Praying in the synagogue, the holy atmosphere during the three meals, and the faces from Szczekociny brought me back to my family home. The memories of the *Shabbat* celebrated with my parents and siblings filled my heart. I was there, back again, trying to taste just a little bit of what my mother was preparing with my oldest sister, unable to resist the tempting smells. By *Shabbat*, delicacies had already filled our house with their smells since Friday morning. They had teased our senses, promising another extraordinary feast coming after simple food weekdays, and we were so impatient to taste some. However, it was difficult to get it. My eldest sister, Sara, kept an eye on everything. Not always did she agree to let us taste *Shabbat* cake. We had no choice but to accept it, though with true disappointment.

I recall Friday rush in the town to finish everything before the holy time came. I remember women doing their last shopping and completing cooking at clean home, and preparing *Shabbat* clothes for all the family. We children would run to the bakery, carrying our pots filled with *Chulent* [1] to have it ready and warm for Saturday. Many had the same pots, so we used to mark them in order to be able to recognize them later on Saturday morning, when we were sent by parents again to bring home our *Chulent*. Funnily enough, many times we would also make the same mark on the pot and thus face a hilarious situation. Never did we make any trouble, however. Politely, all of us would take the smaller pot suggesting, the other person to choose first.

Before dusk, a shames would come and knock at the Jewish door to remind people of the holy time coming; he would also enter Jewish shops and hurry their owners to close, since no work could be done during that time. However, religious merchants, and at that time most of people in the town were religious, knew themselves to close around an hour and a half before. On Saturday evening, on the other hand, Christian customers would gather impatiently waiting to shop. They would knock at the door and windows calling, "You can open! There are already three stars in the sky!"[2]

---

1   *Chulent*, Yiddish, a traditional Jewish stew of potatoes, barley, beans and meat, simmered overnight and eaten for lunch on *Shabbat*

2   According to Jewish tradition, the end of *Shabbat* is marked with three stars appearing in the sky

Even though *Shabbat* was every week, each Friday dusk used to be the same important and ceremonious event. The house was changed into a spotless place; no dust, no dirt. During the week, it was obvious that there was some mess here and there with so many children and work around to do, however, on Friday evening, our house was shining with tidiness. I remember us sitting at the table during holy evenings of *Shabbat* and eating special meals from elegant plates with various ornaments around. This was the best time for us all.

After purifying ourselves in the *Mykve*, we, boys, went with my father to the synagogue. After the ceremony, we wished each other *Shabbat Shalom*, a peaceful *Shabbat*, and with joy and a feeling of holiness, we rushed home. It was a small *shtetl*, so it was close everywhere. When I grew older, we used to meet with other boys for *Oneg Shabbat* [1]. We would pray and sing for a few hours on our own until the regular praying before sunset. It used to give us so much joy and fill our hearts with holiness.

On Friday evening, after coming back from the synagogue, when my mother had already lit the candles and the table had been prepared for a ceremonious dinner, my father used to bless the children. There are special *Shabbat* prayers for boys and girls. My father used to put his hands on our heads, asking God to make his sons like Ephraim and Menasseh and his daughters like Sarah, Rachel, Rebecca, and Leah [2]. Then, we sang *Shalom Alechem* [3]. We welcomed the Angels of Peace, which we believed came from God for holy *Shabbat*. According to a belief, they brought the same *Shabbat* the following week; therefore, we all took care to set everything in right order, proper and clean, so that the next time would also be good and right. Then, finally, we were all sitting at the beautifully laid table with shiny silverware. Obviously, we had separate dishes for meat and separate for dairy, according to Jewish law. My father blessed wine and bread (*Challah*)

---

1   *Oneg Shabbat*, Hebrew, Joy of *Shabbat*; gathering of Jews to express the happiness of the holiday of *Shabbat*, accompanied by joyful praying and singing

2   a traditional *Shabbat* blessing of children performed by parents, who ask God to make their children like their biblical ancestors

3   *Shalom Alechem*, Hebrew, "Peace be upon you," a traditional Friday evening song to welcome in the angels coming to a person's home

that my mother, as other Jewish women, used to bake for each *Shabbat*. We prayed, sang, and ate the delicacies we did not taste during weekdays. We felt the holiness around and inside our hearts. We all, my parents, sisters, and brothers, used to look at one another with merry hearts. Chanting prayers with our father, the beautifully laid table, and the special clothes we wore - it all created a holy atmosphere that filled us all with joy and love to one another.

There were two extraordinary *Shabbat* evenings in my life. One, in the beginning of the nineteen thirties, was when my dear grandmother Esther Rachel Lenczner passed away. I will always remember her inspiring activity and devotion to her grandchildren. Each year before Passover, we saw her renovate the kitchen, repair holes in the walls and paint them with a fresh color and nice pattern. All year round, she helped everybody; she used to sew buttons to our clothes and darn holes in them; she would wash, iron, and fold them perfectly in the closet. She used to prepare tasty food for us and play with us whenever we could. Her funny stories used to make us laugh loudly and heartily, but she would also give us lessons for life, always reminding us to be good people. She taught us love; to fight and win with love. "Remember," she would say, "if somebody throws stones at you, throw them back a piece of bread."

"I love you, all my grandchildren," were her last words when she was sixty-seven, lying in bed on that special Friday evening. "I wish you success and health from the bottom of my heart. Be blessed in the future, work and be good." We all sorely missed her warmth.

Another time also marked the end and the coming of death in our peaceful life, though we couldn't know it at that time. During one of our *Shabbat* dinners in 1937, my father took a newspaper and read to us all what was happening in Europe and how Jews were treated in Germany. We were all horrified and didn't know what to do. We all knew from the Bible how many times the Jewish nation was persecuted, how many times they our faith, our beliefs and traditions, and our lives were at stake, and so it seemed that another period of persecution was coming. We did not know how serious it would be and how we should react or prepare for that.

"I will go and discuss it with the Rabbi," my father decided. "Maybe it would be wiser to sell the houses and all we have and leave for Palestine?" he wondered, and we all sat silently, realizing the situation must have been really serious, if such plans were made.

However, the Rabbi discouraged my father from leaving. "Here is your place," he told him. "You will not be able to fulfill God's commandments anywhere that good as you can do it here, in Poland." It seemed the only right place for Jews in his opinion, as Palestine at that time was to a large extent a secular country, with dominant Zionist, non-religious, immigrants. Thus, my father decided to stay.

Two years later, the war broke out. There were no plans any more beside the endeavors to survive at least one hour more. There seemed no future for us at all.

Nevertheless, the invitation from the Kirshentsweigs and the time spent with them was very pleasant. I experienced a true religious, family atmosphere. It made me feel warm and safe, though at the same time, my heart was tight with yearning for my family and our life together. It made me feel the same pain in knowing that those days would not return, and I was left alone without even knowing what exactly they went through? I was trying to remain satisfied and content with what I had. David, Shoshana's husband was a very good man and insisted he would help me financially. I couldn't accept it, didn't want to make debts without being sure when I would be able to give it back, but I truly appreciated his care.

At that time I came to know Shoshana Graypner, a young and good-looking girl, and David Zalman Lenczner. He used to live in close vicinity of our *Kibbutz*; therefore, we would visit him for *Shabbat*s. Apparently, I wasn't alone. We were all trying to support one another as much as we could, in all possible ways. We could not count on anybody else. Days went by, and I worked hard trying to get used to the new circumstances and to the new world. I was physically strong and felt nothing could discourage me. Though still very fragile inside, I tried to come to terms with reality. I knew I had to begin to build my life, alone and far from the warm place I had left years ago when the war had broken out. I had to forget about all I had known so well, all my adolescent dreams and plans, and I had to start right from the beginning, cautiously setting my feet into the future.

Another Rosh HaShana was approaching, and the thought of leaving the *Kibbutz* forever was growing stronger and stronger inside me. A week before High Holidays I went to my four dear friends, Elisha, Shaya, Moshe, and David.

"Look," I said, "life here in *Kibbutz* is very good for us. We have no worries. We are provided with everything: clothes, food, places to sleep, but we don't have any money." I looked at them, they were listening carefully and probably guessing what I was getting at. "Let's assume we stay here another ten or fifteen years," I continued. "We will have exactly the same things as we have these days. We will be in the same place as we are now. We are rich as *Kibbutz* members, with the houses, the synagogue, all these fields, machines and cars. But it all belongs to the *Kibbutz*, and we, the truth is, have nothing."

They thought about what they heard, looking at me carefully, and one of them asked, "Do you want to leave the *Kibbutz*?" "Yes." I said, determined. "I know it is a challenging decision, but I want to try."

Moshe seemed to follow my way of thinking. Maybe he had already thought about it too. "Listen, Mendel," he said, "I can talk to my sister and her husband. They live in Ramat Gan. Maybe they would be willing to store the beds we are going to get from the Jewish Agency. But anyway it is a difficult task! How do you want to do it? Do you have any plan?"

A discussion resulted, and all of them started to give their opinions and arguments, all at once. I had to wait until they calmed down, making sure they were listening to what I was to say. "We can stay in other *Kibbutzim*. If Moshe's sister agrees, it will be a great help for us. We have now so many friends around, they will be more than happy to spend the holidays with us! And after that, we will start looking for a job. With God's help, we will find one, I am sure. We need to try!"

Filled with excitement and great expectations, we started to get ready with our plan. We had no problem in the *Kibbutz* with borrowing a truck. A driver also agreed to move the beds to Moshe's sister's place. Slowly we were making it. On our leaving, we were assured by the secretarial members, "Our doors are always open for you. Please know that you can always come back if you have difficulties outside. But of course we wish you good luck!" We felt very safe and happy having heard that. The risk did not seem so big now. Reassured in our hearts, right before the holidays, we set off for *Kibbutz* Einat and *Kibbutz* Givat HaSlosha, where we were cordially accepted and where we spent a wonderful time.

We did not wait until the end of the festival period, but we started to walk the streets of Ramat Gan in between the holidays. We entered each and single shop and restaurant, asking if there would be any job for us, anything we could do. In each of them, to our disappointment, we heard a different excuse, "If you had been here last week, I would have had something," or "Come next week. Maybe I will find something for you."

Nevertheless, we did not give up. We knew we had to be persistent. Nobody had promised us it would be easy or quick, and we had taken it into consideration while making the decision to leave. We moved to Givatayim and continued like we did in Ramat Gan. Soon, we came to a tile factory. Maybe here we will be luckier, as they seem to have a lot of work to do here, I thought, looking around. At that time, tiles were becoming more and more popular. People were putting them on the floors in their homes. I went inside with Elisha. All the workers, the manager included, were Yemenites. Looking around the place, we went to the office with the aim of talking to the owner.

"We are immigrants from Poland," we started to explain, but he interrupted us. "From Poland? I am also from Poland. My name is Stutsiner," he introduced himself.

We were somewhat nicely surprised by this coincidence, but it did not necessarily meant we would be get the job. "We are survivors from concentration camps and we are looking for a job," I continued.

"It's hard work. Look," he said, taking us for a walk around the factory.

"I know this job," I said. "I worked in Givat Hashlosha. They also produce tiles there. Please give me a trial period, one week?" I asked him.

He looked at me for a moment, and finally I heard, "OK," to my great happiness. "But only you," he added. "Come tomorrow and we will see."

Although only I was allowed to come and try the work the next day, we were all happy we succeeded at least with that. It was the first step, and we felt we would help each other in any circumstances. For some period of time, I remained the only one who had a job, but it was obvious I would share the salary among us all. We were like brothers to one another. It is rare at times to find such good relations within families, between siblings. We were truly devoted to one another. They would do the same for me. Since I proved to be a good worker, I was allowed after a period of time to bring another friend, and we decided it would be Elisha. It was hard work, as the owner had said in the very beginning, but we were strong and determined. We unloaded cement bags, and produced tiles, respecting the job we had and trying hard to give our best. The manager was very kind and helpful, and he taught us and gave tips on how to be more productive and thus earn more money.

In the meantime, we were contacted by a few other friends from our *Kibbutz*. They had left to build their independent life outside too. We met together and exchanged experiences, and thanks to them we managed to find a flat. It took us some time, all in all, but eventually we all succeeded in our endeavors. Finally, we all had jobs and lived together in the two-asbestos-room apartment, trying to be happy with what we had achieved ourselves. We used to visit our friends we had made in Italy and spend *Shabbat* with them. Most of them got married in the meantime. We would sing and dance together, trying to enjoy our lives we were making.

In December 1947, I was recruited to the army. During that process, it was suggested that I change my name. I was told that Mendel had long time ago become an old-fashioned, *Diaspora*[1] name, not used in Israel. I myself did not think of it that way. This name was given to me by my parents, after my late grandfather, and I felt completely fine about it. The secretary in the

1   *Diaspora*, Greek, a community of people sharing common ethnic and cultural background and living among other communities; here referring to Jews living outside Israel

army who was responsible for all formalities involved had one association: since I was Mendel, she immediately connected it with Menachem Mendel, a character from a famous book at that time by *Shalom Aleichem* [1]. I had no other choice, and I agreed to change my name to Menachem. For my friends, however, I remained forever Mendel, and I felt grateful to them for that. I didn't like my new name. Mendel was my connection with the old world, with my parents, who chose it, and my grandfather, after whom I carried it. This change came as another rebirth in my life. I was born and brought up in Szczekociny as Izyk Mendel; I became a mere prison, number, B-94 for the Nazis during the war, and now, I was starting another chapter, my new life, as Menachem Bornstein, a soldier.

Izyk Mendel Bornstein as a soldier of the Israeli Defense Forces in the 1950-ties, Israel

---

1   *Shalom Aleichem*, a pen name of Russian Jewish writer Sholem Naumovich Rabinovich, (1859 – 1916) an author of Yiddish novels, short stories and plays, upon which the best known are these that gave loose base for the musical Fiddler on the Roof

TWELVE

Our camp was in Sirkin. We were taught protection procedures. The liberation of our country was the utmost goal. Every new weapon that arrived meant a lesson with our commanders, who used to teach us how to dismantle it, clean it, and finally assemble it back. We trained hours in fields. We learned how to throw grenades and soon went on to carry on relatively small actions. The first practice came in Migdal Zedek in Rosh Ha'ayin, where at midnight we blew up a quarry.

Soon I was appointed a group commander, and I took on the training responsibilities. My position was equal to a commander's, and so were my commands. I did my best to perform each task so that everything was flawless. I was proud I was among those protecting my new motherland, though it was difficult to accept the unstable situation, especially for us survivors. After all the killing, hatred, and war atrocities we witnessed in Europe, we had come to our Holy Land to enter yet another crisis. However, it was a kind of purification and rehabilitation for us, too. Now we were given a chance to protect and defend both ourselves and our country with our people.

Many of us after coming here faced the criticism from those who were not survivors. They claimed that we had not fought, that the truth was we had let the oppressors to lead us to death like lambs. It hurt us all deeply. Anyone saying that had no idea of the circumstances we had left behind, how perfectly planned our annihilation was, carried out over time to weaken our bodies with starvation, to bring us down to mere instincts, to threaten and humiliate us each step we took in the closed, limited, and perfectly guarded spaces. They fed us with fear. Intimidated, weak and starving, closed in ghettos, we begged God for a slice of bread, dreading for our closest relatives, uncertain what next days would bring. In such reality, no human can go beyond their survival instincts. Faces with no feelings, evil dogs, guns and watchtowers with cold eyes followed each short step we took, and our reality was that any second our owners could decide our death sentences. In 1939 we entered a huge factory of death. No words and no descriptions, no matter how meticulous and deep, can truly reveal what we had gone through, what our widened eyes saw.

Now we had our chance to prove we were worth something. We could fight and protect not only ourselves but also the new home that we were given, with all its inhabitants. Our roles changed. We felt pride that we were responsible for such important missions. Everybody treated their service seriously and tried hard to perform their duties best as they could.

Soon I was assigned to the Tenth Division and Tenth Brigade. I was an active fighter and I participated in all the missions during the War of Independence in 1948. I was in Tel Ha'shomer, Lod, Ramla, Kfar Salame, Arab Kfar Saba, and Kakun Tantura and many more places. I fought, feeling strong and important as an active commander and fighter with a rifle and a group of subordinate soldiers. I was not afraid of anything and always gave my all. At that time, Arabs attacked us with different bombs and guns, but they also gave up more quickly when their defeat was clear.

During one of the fights in 1947, I was with a group of ten people in one of the Arab villages. There were continuous fights going on. We were especially attacked from one direction, by apparently a very fierce shooter. Suddenly, I had an idea, "Please watch me carefully," I said to my soldiers. "I want to do something, and I will need your help." I started crawling up the mountain toward the direction of the shots fired at us. I waited until he was not looking in my direction, then went up to him from behind and caught him. My soldiers joined me immediately, and we seized him. Later, I got his "Parabellum" rifle from my commandant, who was very proud of me. They published this story in our magazine, and I was treated as a hero.

Nothing ever discouraged me from serving actively my country. I continued my mission and devotion until the fights of 1949, when my left arm was injured quite severely. A shrapnel also hit my face next to the left eye. It was quite a severe wound, but I could see anyway. I was promised plastic surgery by a professional doctor from Africa but found no time to do it and later got used to my scar. I received the bullet from my arm after the surgery to remind me of these days. Fortunately for me, I managed to recover completely, but to my deep disappointment, I was no longer allowed to fight. "I'm sorry," the commander informed me, "According to the law, the fighters need to be classified as A-1. You will be placed into non-combat positions."

I couldn't help the feeling of shame being born inside me. I was so proud of being a fighter, and it had come to an end so quickly! I treated it as a failure. I would have never suspected I would have to give up my position as a fighting soldier. Now, I needed to find my new mission in serving others.

This is how I decided to take a preventive medicine course. The 1950s was a time of many arrivals to the Holy Land. Many immigrants were coming from Aden, Yemen, Algeria, Morocco, and Tunisia. Many were coming from European countries too: Hungary, Romania, France, Belgium, and Poland. According to the procedures, their blood was tested to prevent any spread of diseases. I was, therefore, sent to the Lod Airport, where I spent a month-and-a-half taking blood from their fingers and checking it carefully. After several months of living in tents, the immigrants started to complain about mosquitoes and lice. The Head of the Preventive Medicine Unit assigned me to this job to prevent the suffering of the immigrants. I was to train a group of soldiers to carry out this mission flawlessly, and equipped with disinfectants, I was sent to the place.

As I looked at the immigrants, my memory brought me images from my camp life during the war years. I knew well what lice meant; I had lived with them for many years. In the beginning, Nazis took care of it and tried to eliminate it, but toward the end of the war, it was completely disregarded. Here, the immigrants were living in good conditions. Tents were only a temporary solution before they were moved to housing blocks that were built for them. The government tried hard to organize their living according to acceptable standards. Yet, I couldn't help the associations born in my mind when I was fighting off the insects disturbing their lives.

At that time, I was working in the clinic with Dr. Sivroni in Camp Dura. During one of our first conversations, I learned that he was from Kielce, Poland. My heart started to beat faster. Maybe he knows something of my family! I thought. Though Kielce was not a small *shtetl* as my Szczekociny, I hoped by some twist of fate he might know something about my siblings. Right away, it turned out he did not know them, but he was close to my father's sister, Rachel Goldblum, and was dating her daughter, my cousin, Lola! According to what he knew, Lola had survived the Holocaust and moved to Venezuela. He was still in touch with their accountant and thus was able to provide me with their address. I couldn't believe my luck. Not only did I learn that a member of my close family was still alive, but I was given an opportunity to contact them! I was so happy and excited. I wrote to Lola immediately, attaching a picture of her brother, David, that I had received from the accountant. I did not have to wait a long time for a reply. In her great joy, Lola decided to come to Israel with both her daughters and her husband. Our meeting was one of the most touching moments I experienced after the war. Years would prove our contact was not temporary. We would meet in Israel every year, where she would come to visit me, until her demise in 1982. Her two daughters moved with their families to United States, where they work in clinics as a cancer specialist and a psychologist, respectively.

I remain deeply thankful to Fate for putting me in touch with Dr. Sivroni. Not only did he love me like his son, providing me with wonderful working conditions. It is thanks to him I started to feel at that time less lonely and abandoned. He brought me my close relatives, and it happened in the time when I had already lost any hopes of finding any member of my family alive.

In the 1950s, the decision came to move the General Headquarters Unit to a different location. I did not even think about changing the place; I had already gotten used to the new conditions and felt very good where I was. However, I had no other option when one day I was informed I was going away for two months, since they needed someone from Medical Forces to arrange the new place. There is no refusal in the army, but I did it with a heavy heart. There, I was responsible for inspecting kitchens, dining halls, storerooms, and the doctor's unit, taking care soldiers got fresh food and the places were hygienic. Everybody knew me, and I felt the importance of what I was doing. What will become here without me? I thought about my new situation, a little worried.

After two months of my new duties, when I was happily getting ready to go back to Zrifin, I was shocked to hear from Commander Dafni, "Buddy, you are staying here! Don't worry about anything." He reassured me, seeing my confusion, "Everything will be arranged for you." So it happened. There I stayed until retirement due to my age, in 1968. The army authorities did not want to accept my decision at first to let me go.

"Please understand me," I said, turning to them. "I want to go when I am still quite young. All my life I have been under instructions. I did not have a regular childhood. I want to make up for it a little." Then, I became a member of Reserved Forces Society.

I felt that the time had come to focus more on my private life. I felt I had experienced enough, I was grateful for that period of my life, and wanted to focus on a different aspect of my life. My army service was an eventful period, filled with variety of emotions, from fear during the military operations, through sorrow over lost battles and dead comrades, joy and affection over victories, until pride of serving Jewish country and protecting its people.

I remember very well the April military Operation "Nachshon," during the civil war of 1947 – 1948. Palestinian Arabs blocked the Jerusalem road, and our objective was to open it and to supply the Jewish community in Jerusalem with food and water. Our aim was to enable the convoy of trucks escorted by armored military cars to enter Jerusalem and bring essential ingredients and food supplies to the Jewish people there. I was among the soldiers lying with weapons in the mountains, keeping our eyes on the situation. The convoy was long indeed, almost all the way from Tel Aviv to Jerusalem. At some point of time, I was taken by my squad commander into his armored car with my first aid kit. We were proceeding slowly, when suddenly an Arab truck showed up. These were the longest minutes of my life. I was not sure what would happen, while the enemy truck, which was much bigger, tried hard to push us off the road. I felt my heart was going to break through my chest with its strong beats, and I was overwhelmed with fear. After the moments of struggle, the commandant miraculously managed to drive the truck into a ditch, and we took a while there trying to calm down as we watched the truck disappear. Later, I was pride and happy that again the difficult and risky mission ended successfully and we reached our people in the Holy City, able to help them.

After these events, all the country people remained apprehensive and vigilant, concerned our enemies would be willing to attack us again. At the same time, everybody tried to live their everyday lives no matter what was happening around. It was my turn in the army to go on vacation; we had planned the holiday schedule carefully to suit each soldier's wish. I was sitting with my wife and children in the car, setting off for our long expected holidays, when we were stopped with the news coming from the loudspeakers: all the vacations were cancelled due to the emergency situation; all the soldiers are requested to come back to their positions until further notices. I became overwhelmed with deep dissatisfaction and sadness. I could not look at my wife and children and I felt their disappointment and disbelief. We all knew it would certainly be almost impossible to organize that event again. Yet, I had committed to serve faithfully and loyally and I knew the meaning of these words. I was aware of the situation, of the enemy around, and all the perils resulting from this fact. No hardship would make me regret my decision to serve what I considered to be my new homeland. I only wished my dear family, my greatest treasure, would not have to bear any unpleasant consequences of my commitment. I wanted to protect them, and save them from any inconvenience.

Even more fearful for my family had I become during the *Six Day War*, fought between Israel, and Egypt, Jordan, and Syria[1], in 1967, when the threat came that Israel would be attacked by the four surrounding Arab countries, heavily and professionally armed with the best and newest weapons and gases from Russia. I was particularly compassionate toward mothers, who dreaded for their babies. "How do you put a respirator on a baby?" they kept asking, worried. "The respirator itself can kill a baby!" I was so sorry that they had to go through it. I still had in my mind and heart all the women, children, and babies who perished in the Holocaust. I remembered the dreadful stories I heard of babies thrown into fire, out of houses, at trains, all with their mothers being forced to watch before they were murdered themselves. Again, I faced the injustice toward the most innocent and fragile; nobody would certainly attack them in that way, but still the fear and suffering was strong.

We had lived for a while with the hope that Levi Eshkol, the Prime Minister at that time, would keep his promise not to start any fighting actions unnecessarily. Eventually however, the King of Jordan joined Egypt and the

---

1 *Six Day War*, Arab - Israeli War, fought between Israel, and Egypt, Jordan and Syria supported by other Arab forces; as a result of which Israel gained control of the Sinai Peninsula, the Gaza Strip, the West Bank, East Jerusalem and Golan Heights. It has affected the geopolitics until these days

war broke out. The losses were great on both sides, people stayed at home glued to their radio stations to hear the news. The phone in the clinic did not stop ringing. Parents, wives, and close relatives were apprehensive and kept inquiring about their children, husbands, and their closest relatives and friends. I understood and supported them completely during the whole period. I remained patient and calm, trying to explain everything according to the orders I received. I kept reassuring and encouraging worried families. Fortunately, the great day of victory came, and I felt proud and touched to serve in IDF, which could be trusted and that made us safe and secure. There was a great and overwhelming happiness after the *Six Day War*. People hugged one another in the streets, danced, sang, and cried with joy. Many secular people turned religious, as a result of what they perceived as divine intervention. It was a truly unique event in our country and our hearts. All around, voices were heard shouting joyful exclamations: "Rabin King of Israel lives forever!" Rabbi Goren, Chief Rabbi of IDF, blew the horn at the *Western Wall* [1].

The situation brought about the world's attention. Many praised the IDF's great actions and bravery. Within the headquarters of IDF, the victory was celebrated with a special expedition that was organized a few months later. We, the IDF senior officers, traveled along the Negev Desert and Dead Sea in a convoy of heavy military trucks.

After several days of short stops for simple meals and short nights of sleeping on the bare ground, guarded by military men, we finally reached our destination - Mount Sinai. Because of our tiredness from the long journey, there was not a strict order that told us to climb the top of the mountain, and some of the people decided to stay. Others resigned during the three-hour climb onto the high mountain of three thousands steps. I was one of the three hundred who started the climbing and among the thirty who did not give up until the end. There, on the top, we found a monastery with a rich library of books written in seventy languages, electricity, water, and food supplies. We met 110 servants and their masters there, and ten monks, who reminded me of *Chassid*s, with their long beards and gowns.

1   *Western Wall*, Wailing Wall or *Kotel*, an important Jewish religious site located in the Old City of Jerusalem, the remaining *Western Wall* of the Second Temple, gathering Jews from all over the world for prayers, usually written on pieces of paper and left in the crevices of the stones

Twelve

Although I had difficulties walking for three days and it was a challenging and exhausting time, it did not even cross my mind not to go up. I could have even been the first or one of those first. However, approximately thirty meters before the goal, I heard behind my back the call of Major General Shemuel Eyal. "Sergeant Menachem! Wait a moment!" I stopped to listen to him. "Please, let me be the first to reach the destination." I considered it an honor to fulfill his request and to follow him with a flag we waved. The picture taken at that moment, up on top of the Mount Sinai, reminds me of all the emotions which filled our hearts during the whole expedition.

I felt pride of my country and its army, as much as gratitude to God for the outcome and the sadness that I had to experience another war, another tragedy, another suffering of victims. I couldn't understand how come happened again, short after the cruelties and atrocities created by Nazi regime. The world did not apparently learn the lesson, and we were far from peace. And we survivors, after all we went through in Europe, had been endangered again; again we had felt insecure, unstable, attacked. The situation was under control, there was nationwide happiness, but we all knew it was temporary. Though we agreed to give away the territories that our enemy demanded, it did not lead to the long awaited peace. I pray there will be no wars anymore, anywhere in our world and nobody will have to suffer, live in insecurity and fear. I pray in my heart that harmony and agreement will finally come to this precious, special land, where so much blood had already been shed.

My army involvement remained an essential part of my life forever. It changed my life and added sense to my survival, which I began to perceive as a debt I had to pay back to the world and humanity. Finally, I was building lasting friendships. Of course there were losses during the fights; there was still a level of apprehension and insecurity, but it cannot even be compared with the fear with which I had been filled with in the concentration camps. I really loved being a soldier and all the work I performed in the army. I never resigned from any fight or refused any order I was given; an order was always an order for me, even if I did not like or understand it or if I found it a surprise. Though I encountered many difficult moments on my soldier's way, I never thought of leaving the army. It became my life mission, to serve my new homeland, to protect its people, never to allow for anything that would be similar to what I had come through in Europe. It had always remained painful and difficult for me to accept the fact that after the tragedy and suffering of the Holocaust, there were still fights and wars in the world. We Jews could not live safely and calmly. I actively served as a fighter and medic during the most important fights and wars in the history of the State of Israel. During my service, there were moments of danger and risk to our lives, times that threatened the entire country, and painful losses, but there were also touching moments that filled us with pride and the strength to continue.

Despite all the possible difficulties and dangers, I trusted IDF completely with all its decisions, and I felt safe in the country it was protecting. This small piece of land, suffering from numerous wars and attacks through thousands of years, just like its children, was the only place we felt it belonged to us, Jews. After all the humiliation and dehumanization I had gone through in camps, I became an active and proud soldier, not only trying to perform my duties best as I could, but also always trying to think of possible improvements I could introduce to make our army life better.

One of my main army responsibilities was taking care of soldier blood donation. This was not easy, as most of people do not like to donate blood. Most of the soldiers used to come with the fear that they could faint or even die after giving blood. "Listen," I said, trying to calm them down. "Donating your blood once in a while is good for your circulation. It energizes your blood. After a few weeks, you get back both the amount and quality of what you donated." I was always an example for them. They would watch me while I lay calmly, with my blood flowing to a syringe. After three minutes when the 300cc test tube was full, I would stand up with a smile and have a cup of coffee. Despite all my efforts, very few soldiers volunteered, even though there was quite a big demand from those who were wounded.

I thought a lot about possible solutions to the problem and finally reported back to my commander, Lieutenant-Colonel Dafni Aharon. Tough and pedantic as he might have been perceived, he did not forget to appreciate those, who were trying hard using their talents and were performing their duties well praising them with all the benefits and privileges they deserved. As his subordinate, I felt proud I was given to work with him.

"The situation is not good," I said, "Something needs to be done to encourage soldiers to participate." I had a suggestion.

"We could give one day off to each donor and a guarantee that if they or their family receive wounds within a year, they have the right to receive three blood units."

Both he and the headquarters accepted my suggestion and, in a short period of time, it proved to be working. I continued to reduce their fear and was always the first to donate. I remember this each time when I look at my behavior sheet that each Israeli soldier receives on being recruited, and which is filled with comments on their discipline, performance of their duties etc. Mine is filled on both sides, in large, red letters: Blood donation for IDF soldiers.

Upgrading the blood donation process was only one of numerous enhancements that came from my side. I issued numerous orders concerning food storage and usage, making sure soldiers got fresh food and that food that had passed the expiration date was properly handled. A few times during my regular inspections, I noticed fresh loaves of bread lying in the garbage room in a disposal bag. I wasn't sure what to think about it until one day I saw a man loading them onto a pickup truck.

"What are you doing with this bread?" I wanted to know.

"I am taking it for animals in my *Kibbutz*," he explained. "I leave some money in return to the officials." He looked at me carefully as if surprised, trying perhaps to understand why I had asked. I stood there, and I couldn't say a word as I tried to come to terms with what I learned. Fresh bread was thrown in disposal bags and then taken for animals to prevent it from becoming complete waste - unbelievable.

"I used to be an officer too," he added. "I retired some time ago."

His voice brought me back to earth. I replied something to him and went away, thinking about what to do. I couldn't believe the army was getting rid of fresh bread in disposal bags, with no respect, while so many people in the world, in this country even, did not have enough to eat. I decided to make an immediate appointment with the unit commander.

"Sir," I said to Dafni Aharon seriously, "I'm having a truly hard time trying to come to terms with a certain situation." I explained to him all the circumstances of what I saw. "I am coming from concentration camps, where a piece of old, decayed, and dry bread was a dream for us, a treasure that meant postponing the death sentence we all were facing. Even today, there are still people in this country that are starving. I really think it is not right that we treat food this way. Having starved for years, I cannot look at fresh bread being kept in the garbage room, wasted, and thrown away or left for animals. It seems unbelievable!"

The commander listened patiently until the end, "Well," he said, "according to the general headquarters' rules, there are portions specified for each soldier. Some of them don't eat in our canteen; some prefer other food than bread. This is what it looks like?"

I knew there were parties held here almost twice a week with a special budget; people order meat and sausages. I suggested reducing the amount of bread and, instead making more meat, soldiers should be given larger meat portions for lunch to keep them eating here and not waste any food.

To my satisfaction, the idea was accepted, and I could become calm no bread would be taken for granted. What is more, I received a small amount of money as a prize for my suggestion, which came as a complete surprise to me. I did not expect anything but the right attitude toward food, bread especially, which still meant so much for many.

I learned that, unfortunately, many times we have to lose what we have in order to appreciate it. Bread will always mean more to me than it does to others. There was a time I could only crave it, almost having forgotten its taste. That time in Plaszow I risked my life to fill my stomach with just a few pieces of it. It took a long time to get used to the amounts of food I saw after the liberation. I had already forgotten there could be such a variety and such amounts of edibles! Even after many years, my grown children used to joke that the size of the sandwiches I prepared for them were always beyond their capabilities of opening the mouths. I never came back to the state of mind from before the war. Having experienced years of starvation; having seen people eating grass and even pieces of the bodies of their dead comrades to stay alive; having bones protruding from my thirty-kilogram body myself, it will forever bother and sadden me to see people waste, disrespect or throw away what still can be eaten, just as it bothers me to hear them complain about what they have to eat.

There was another issue that bothered me. It concerned women soldiers from our unit. Unlike us men, they stayed in hotels, which seemed not only a lack of proper organization, but it must have cost the army a lot of money. At the same time, during my careful and frequent inspections, I got to know the surroundings well and knew there were some pieces of land staying unused. Soon after the event with the bread, I came to talk to the commander again.

"Sir, it is not connected to my profession or qualifications, therefore you may well reject my suggestion, but I will appreciate it if you listen to it. I was thinking a lot about the spacious land the army owns. Why not build wooden cabins there for women soldiers? It would be much more convenient for the army, and at the same time, the cost of building them would equal a yearly payment for the hotels. The cabins are easy and quick to build and will stay for years."

The commandant promised to think about it and talk at the headquarters. To my satisfaction and contentment, soon the cabins were built, and women soldiers could move in. The commander was happy again to inform me that I would receive a prize again.

I never expected anything in return for what I did; I was always driven by a genuine wish to improve the conditions within my environment, and it made me happy to see my suggestions accepted, introduced into life, and, eventually, working for us all. Though the gifts were pleasant, they were secondary to me. Only the fact that I helped and did something good to better the existence of us all was enough and filled me with satisfaction. At the same time, I must admit that such situations helped me rebuild my level of self-esteem and made me feel more confident and stronger. It was there, in the army, that I learned and came to deeply believe that one man can make a difference. Each of us is born with chances to improve the environment around us. We are provided numerous opportunities no matter the circumstances and details we experience. The improvements in the army that were introduced due to my initiatives came as solely my own suggestions and ideas. I did not leave them aside but tried to make them real with the help of my superiors. The willingness to serve, help and improve; to react to injustice and to simply contribute to building a better world remained with me forever.

The cover of the certificate of release from the Israeli Defense Force service

1589	בורנשטיין	מנחם
מס׳ אישי	שם משפחה	שם פרטי

תאריך שחרור 30 . 8.68	אורך שרות	שנים 20	חדשים 6	מס׳ זהות 234414

דרגות בעת השחרור	זמנית: /	קבע: רס"ן

מקצועות צבאיים שנרכשו (המקבילים למקצועות אזרחיים)	שם המקצוע משק תברואה	סוג 08

עיטורים אותות וציונים לשבח	אות מלחמת ששת הימים

ההתנהגות (חוגרים בשרות חובה בלבד)	/	דירוג ההתנהגות : טובה מאד טובה מניחה את הדעת אינה מניחה את הדעת

סיבת השחרור	תהל"ק

הערכה	/

קצ"ב 377256/ אירש חנה

תעודה מס׳ № 172405 חותמת	חתימה תאריך 12.1.69

The inside of the certificate of release from the Israeli Defense Force service

THIRTEEN

My journey back comes to an end. I think of all the doubts I used to have before coming to my hometown, Szczekociny, and though they are still close to me, I do not have regrets. I look gratefully at my dear family. I am thankful that they encouraged me to come here and that they supported me all the way. I feel that my journey could not happen before, and all the pieces had to come together. I had to come to discover the devastation, to discover my mission and duty for those who were no longer alive and who could not speak for themselves. I was brought back here by the crying of the desecrated souls who could not rest in peace. We will not leave it and will not rest until the toilets are removed, and the monument commemorating the Jews from Szczekociny is built. We all agree this is the only way for proper use of the crashed tombstones from the Jewish cemeteries. We feel it as an obligation to memorialize thousands of Jewish people who used to live in Szczekociny with their Christian neighbors for hundreds of years. We came in the moment when most of the people had already forgotten them, and some never heard of. Not only their gravestones were removed from their right places, and used for building purposes, many times trodden on day by day, lying silently among other stones, and forced to serve as pavement. The bones of these people cannot any longer rest peacefully in their cemeteries, where years ago they had been buried by their families. They had disappeared somewhere in the rubbish with which they were mixed. The memory of all these generations of Jews had almost disappeared, and, sadly, probably in a few years it would go away finally with the last living witnesses.

I leave Szczekociny and inside I am changed again. Though sad and devastated with what I saw, at the same time I feel more strength, as if I am empowered with extra energy. I leave with a strong decision to act. After all, I m a believer that one man can make a difference. Apart from all the emotions and memories, I bring with me the birth certificates of my brothers and sisters. It is a true treasure for me. They don't have their gravestones, and their names, all those years, have not been mentioned elsewhere than in my memory. These documents are signed by my father who each time his child was born would come with a witness to certify this fact. Now these pieces of paper certify the fact of existence of my dear siblings.

After coming back home, my son, Yossi, starts writing letters. We ask for support and intervention in our important mission. We write first of all to the mayor of Szczekociny, but there is no reaction. We then ask for help from the World Jewish Congress and other important organizations and figures, such as the Embassy of Poland and Polish Cardinal Macharski. For a long time, it seems we are alone on the battlefield, and our endeavors prove fruitless. The breakthrough comes when Bobby Brown, the director of International Affairs at the World Jewish Congress, sends a letter to the President of Poland, Aleksander Kwasniewski, where he shares our belief: "We believe that righting this wrong would set an example of reconciliation and righteousness that would have a loud resonance beyond Polish-Jewish circles alone. Let Szczekociny become a place that symbolizes hope for the future and remembrance of the past and not feelings of bitterness and estrangement that have too often dominated relations between our peoples." We are also helped by the head of Jewish Community of Katowice District, Mr. Kac. Finally, the President of Poland issues his important decision: the toilets must be taken down.

The private house and the ruins of public toilets in the ground of old Jewish cemetery, Szczekociny, 2006

Before it happened, however, since we are unable to gain any cooperation from the Municipality authorities in Szczekociny, my son, Yossi organizes a delegation visit to Szczekociny. Together with Holocaust survivors: Yehudit Gold, Cela Greenberg, David Richt, Esther Nir, and Shoshana Licht, and second and third generation survivors. There is a protest at the public toilets building. They have Israeli flags with them, and they feel truly touched and agitated with what they discover. It is already two years since my visit to the town, and nothing has changed; therefore, we need to act decisively. There are media accompanying the demonstration. The survivors are interviewed, and there is a wide interest in the town. Some local person is clearly against the presence of survivors there. He brings with himself a coffin layer with the words: "Last farewell," and makes unpleasant remarks. According to his words, he clearly wishes the demonstrators to be buried there, with their ancestors.

The mayor, Mr. Grycner, also attends the event. The authorities claim it is impossible to specify the exact borders of the cemetery, which is supposed to be a justification for the building, as well as preserving the toilets on the place. However, during the event, while people are expressing their protest, to their shock the working excavator digs out some bones. Yossi insists the works are stopped immediately. They bury the remains back, light a candle, and demand the mayor act immediately. Finally, they achieve success with their pleas. The entrance to the toilets is bricked up, before their final destruction.

July 22, 2006, two years after our visit and our discovery of this sad devastation, comes as a very important date on our calendars. The toilets are demolished, and we feel calmer. No more excrement is poured on the holy ground and dear remains of our ancestors. It is at the same time sad we could not reach a peaceful compromise with the local authorities, but were forced to look for support around the world, knocking at different doors; though at times we were not listened to there either. I feel half of our mission is completed. My dream is to see a monument there, to commemorate thousands of Szczekociny Jews who not only perished in the Holocaust but who lived in this *shtetl* for long years, contributing to its shape, who built houses there, traded, brought goods, organized social life by creating banks and libraries and who simply made their lives there. Also, still the private house is stands there, on the remains of our ancestors. People walk and drive their cars on them. It still bothers my heart deeply. What should be done?

In the meantime, Fate comes with support again. I meet Sean Foer, a young student from my neighborhood, who reads my story in one of the newspapers and wants to meet me for an interview, which will appear in his short movie he is to make for school. We spend long hours together. He and his mother, Lisa, listen attentively and with understanding to my difficult life stories. I do not hide them anymore. Though they are still painful to articulate, I realize how important they are. The fruit of our meetings becomes a touching movie Sean prepares about me, entitled *The Spirit of the Survivor*. Sean and Lisa embark on my mission here in the United States. We speak in synagogues, and during various anniversary days, and the story of my survival and of Szczekociny is heard by more and more people. They become truly interested and touched by it. During all these events, we ask for financial contributions for the aim of the monument. We thank each donor with the DVD of Sean's movie. I am deeply touched by their invaluable support. I did not even dream about it; it would have been much more difficult without them. Sean is merely fourteen, but his interest in my life story and his professionalism are as great as his maturity. We manage to collect some sum of money; it is only the tip of the iceberg but the process continues.

At the same time, good news reaches us from Szczekociny. Although still formally it seems a long way to raise the monument, despite the promise from the mayor, important activities start to take place there. The principal deputy of the local secondary school starts a project aimed at restoring the memory of the town's Jewish population. Together with lecturers from Jagiellonian University in Krakow, specializing in Jewish culture, he writes a book of the history of Jews in Szczekociny. Thanks to his cooperation with Yossi, they manage to put together students from Israel and Szczekociny, who research the stories of the town's Jewish survivors.

During one of his continuous visits to the town, Yossi is told there are a few fragments of the *Torah* from the Szczekociny synagogue that have been found at a local family's house. With the help of Miroslaw Skrzypczyk, my son manages to regain those few, visibly weakened with time, but still so precious manuscripts. He takes one fragment and starts reading it, to witness one of the most touching turns of fate during this mission. The fragment he finds happens to be the *Parasha* [1] he used to learn for his *Bar Mitzvah*. Yet even more astonished do we become in June, when my other son, Zvi, takes another of the three found fragments, and this happens to be the *Parasha* he read during his first formal praying in the synagogue on the same occasion. It seems as if we are participating within some bigger project, controlled by some Higher Power. Everything comes to its right place, matching our personal history.

I cannot believe such profound changes took place over a mere four years; it seems a single stone began a whole avalanche of positive events. I am truly happy and touched about each and every step taken within the process of restoring the town's Jewish memory, which I deeply believe contributes to bringing back eternal peace and resting to its inhabitants. I know Szczekociny is not the only town, unfortunately, which forgot its Jewish past. It can, however, be the first with such a deep change. It can set an example of righting a wrong, which never comes too late. My dream is that other *shtetls* will follow.

Finally, as a kind of crowning to all the events that had taken place meanwhile, June 2008, comes with the first Festival of Jewish Culture in Szczekociny. I am one of three survivors to reach the town on that occasion, there are children and grandchildren of others accompanying us too. Just like four years ago, I come with my whole family, this time without the need to be encouraged. I feel truly proud and happy God led to such turn of events. I am asked to speak during the ceremony, after the screening of Sean's movie *The Spirit of the Survivor.* "First of all I thank God for bringing us to this moment," I tell the audience, thanking those who supported my mission on its long way.

We gather at the place where the toilets used to stand. Many local people come; there is the Chief Rabbi of Poland, Michael Schudrich and the representatives of the Municipality in Szczekociny. I stand in front of them

---

1   *Parasha*, a Hebrew word meaning "section"; refers to the division of the five books of Moses, that are read each week

all and say *kaddish* for the entire Jewish community of Szczekociny. My voice trembles. I see tears in the eyes of the listeners, Jewish and Christian alike. After a few words, we are lavished with heavy rain. I look up and remember standing in the dense forest in Gunskirchen, when I told my comrades: "It is not rain. Heaven is crying." I feel the same now. After a few minutes, the sky clears and for the rest of the day the sun keeps shining. We light candles and put stones as a sign of remembering Szczekociny Jews.

We walk through the town and I tell the story of the synagogue and *Mykve*. Now, at the Festival, I reach the place where it used to stand; four years ago I could not remember the exact location. I see this place as it used to be before the war came, the street constantly full of Jews coming for purification of their bodies and souls. At that time, there was no running water at homes. During weekdays in warm seasons, most people, and we as well, used to go to the small pond that was in Szczekociny. The water there was really clean and besides, it was a pleasant place with many trees around. My mother and sisters, like other women, used a big bowl in the kitchen, where they poured water, and washed themselves. All of us however would come to the *Mykve* for deep purification. Women used to come also before getting married each month after their menstruation days finished. Men visited it on Friday afternoons before *Shabbat* and on the eves of other holidays. Each Friday afternoon, we used to come with my father to the *Mykve* to purify our bodies and souls in running water and to prepare for the holy celebration. Only after that did we feel proper enough to enter our temple to pray.

Mykve, our ritual bath, used to be quite a large place with two pools filled with cold and hot water respectively. It could be so hot in one part of it that one could feel as if in a sauna. There were small wooden buckets, which used to come in handy when people wanted to cool themselves or remove the remains of soap. People used branches with leaves on their hot bodies to improve their blood circulation and feel better. Thus, to be humorous, if a student met his teacher there, he could in this way take revenge for bad marks by "accidentally" hitting the teacher.

Now, long years after, there is no sign of the *Mykve*. I tell its story to the public, but we stand in front of a new building. We continue the significant stroll, tracing the town's Jewish history. Before we reach the last stage, we stop at my home. I look around and see true interest and empathy in the eyes surrounding me, while I tell them of my childhood spent here. Finally, we arrive at the parish yard. It is a truly symbolic step. It is here that the Jews of Szczekociny were gathered in September 1942 and taken onto their last journey, right to Treblinka. All of them were dressed in their best clothes for their most important festival, *Yom Kippur*. While my son, Yossi, tells this story to those gathered here, I think about my dear father, who at the same time was shot dead in Wodzislaw. He shared the fate of most of Szczekociny Jews.

I am truly touched with the behavior of the locals. People come over and express their words of approval. They ask me to sign the book written by Miroslaw Skrzypczyk and the lecturers from Jagiellonian University. We go with Kazimiera for a walk around the palace, just like dozens of years ago. In the afternoon, a concert devoted to the memory of Szczekociny Jews starts. Zvika, my son, also appears at the stage. He dedicates me a song about a man who keeps returning, and he speaks about my return from the ashes of the Holocaust. I am deeply touched and proud listening to him singing *Shalom Alechem* to his self composed melody. "Over sixty years ago, there was a little boy walking to the synagogue with his father," Zvika says from the stage, "The angels are following him wherever he goes, and they are here with him tonight." He comes toward me, takes my hand and continues walking with me to the stage.

Izyk Mendel Bornstein with his childhood friend and neighbor, Kazimiera Wojtasinska, now Dobrzyniewicz, in front of the Palace in Szczekociny, 2008

Izyk Mendel Bonstein, in front of his house building, rebuilt after the war, telling his story to the participants of the first Szczekociny Festival of Jewish Culture, 2008

I am standing there thinking how unpredictable life can be. Once, years back, I wouldn't have dared to think I could ever come back here; when I did, and my heart became saddened, in my wildest dreams I did not think a day would come when I would be standing next to my son on the stage, participating in the Festival of Jewish Culture. I am looking at all those people who gathered there on that special day. I want to believe they all understand us, and we are starting a new chapter of our relations.

I remember having heard so many times as a boy here in Poland, "Jews, go to Palestine! There is your place!" It became a kind of slogan for those who believed our existence in Poland was not grounded. As if we were not Polish! Having survived the Nazi-directed hell, we decided to come to the land of Palestine, not knowing the place and anybody there, not having anybody to support us. It seemed at that time to be the only place that we, Jews, could claim as our land. Europe, our thousand-year-old home no longer wanted us. Unfortunately, the end of the war did not liberate the minds of many Europeans, who had been fed hatred towards our culture for a long time. They were still, many times, antagonistic and hostile. Persecutions were still taking place. We could not come back to our family homes, even had we been brave enough to face the presence of this emptiness, that loud silence after the brutally quenched lives of our relatives.

Bitter irony was, however, coming through. We were not wanted in Europe, which said: "Jews to Palestine!" At the same time, we could not enter it, as its borders were protected by the British Army. We had to come illegally. After all the suffering and atrocities we had encountered, we had to face not only the fact we were alone but also that there was no place for us in this world any more. We felt trapped. The Holocaust and loss of my family was the first attack to my safe world. Never would I have expected that after this unimaginable experience I would have to still struggle with further blows.

The persistence of survival force, and desire to leave the old world, which we felt had betrayed us, was, however, strong enough to cover other feelings. Driven by the hope of safety and our new lives to build in the Holy Land, we did everything we could and were told to set our feet there. With time, I understood the humiliation around this process; being forced to travel as an illegal cargo with chickens, uncertain what the outcome would be and if we would be caught by the British Army. And still it was not the end. Still, we had to face the blow from our brothers, other Jews, who were saved the experience of the Holocaust but gave themselves all rights to call us cowards and a faint-hearted flock of sheep. For a long time many treated us as strangers or worse, people of category B, no matter how involved we were in fights protecting what we perceived as our nation. I was bitterly sad, wondering how long we would have to suffer from such insults and humiliation. Wasn't the six-year horror enough? Why did even our own comrades attack us?

Yet, the strong spirit of survivors did not let us lose hearts completely. The children of Israel, finally in this holy land, were singing We are Pioneers and found joy and pride in building the Jewish State against the obstacles. Each helping hand had its role on numerous levels of this construction. I realized many of the important figures in that process were Polish Jews, Ben Gurion, the first Prime Minister of the State Israel included, and I was proud and touched to be one of them. Here we came to start again, removed from certain places nearly from history as well. Looking back, thousands of years, our civilization has constantly suffered and never could we feel secure enough. The enemy was always around the corner ready to attack our Jewishness. It seems to be inscribed into our culture - to be persecuted, hated and forced to leave from where we tried to build our homes. The attack was aimed at our women and children alike, at our temples and religion. We witnessed the collapse and decay of numerous ancient traditions that were rising together with ours. We watched many come and go, yet, certainly to the disappointment of many, we were still here, never giving up, always persisting and no matter how severely decimated, always coming back out of the ashes and starting again. My fate, as other survivors, may well represent the fate of my nation. The enemy attacked harshly again with a meticulous plan of obliteration, which was nearly successful. And again we were saved. We rose again, rebuilding our essence and regrowing our trees. We came back to the land of our ancestors, symbolically coming to the roots.

Was Israel our true homeland yet? What about what we had left behind? Poland itself was home to over three million Jews. I still feel deep connection with this place, though it came to represent a painful grave for me. It is still the place I came to life, where I grew up as a cheerful boy and learned my first steps in so many fields. My heart will always remain a bleeding wound yearning for this once peaceful world.

Maybe it is true? Maybe the home and motherland for us Jews is memory and longing?

The house I was brought up in is still there. It does not belong to us however. It will remain the most precious and most symbolic place for me, bringing my heart a variety of profound emotions, from warmth, love, and safety I experienced as a child there, to the pain and suffering at being forced to leave it forever. It is where everything started for me, and where it finished so suddenly. It is the place to which I am deeply attached, with all my heart, where I gave my first cry, where I opened my eyes, where I put my first steps, where I was brought up among my siblings, where I learned the world. This was my safe shelter, the womb from which I was brutally pulled out of, thrown out into the hostile world, though I had not yet grown.

Recently, in my dreams I see my family more and more: my mother, my father, all my brothers and sisters. We are in a kind of field. I am not sure, but it may be a cemetery. Is it the one in Szczekociny? Does it mean something more? I wake up terrified, because I cannot find my dear wife there.

I close my eyes. It hurts so much to remember, yet I cannot and do not want to forget. Szczekociny. The name moves all my senses. Images are running through my mind, touching my heart so deeply. Such a small place can mean so much. I see my family living our modest, peaceful life, just like hundreds of other Jewish families in our peaceful *shtetl*, befriended by our Christian neighbors. I see the market square surrounded with Jewish houses, quiet during the week and so cheerfully hectic on Wednesdays, filled with various smells and noises of bargaining. I hear the music coming from upstairs during the wedding parties held in our house and quarrels of innocent drunkards from the restaurant opposite the street. Friday knocking at Jewish doors to remind the people that holy *Shabbat* was coming, and after, the impatient Saturday calls of Christian friends asking us to open our shops. I witness the holy silence of *Shabbat* in the streets. I can smell challas and cakes baked on Fridays in our Jewish homes. I see pots with

Chulent at the bakery. *Chanukah* candles in the windows. Children making their own masks for *Purim*. Feathers spread around in the park of the palace.

Never after did I experience the same taste of food I used to eat in my *shtetl*: fruits that used to grow in the forest near the palace; the kidney beans with small spots on them, latkes that were brought for us to school, apples from Kazimiera's garden. I can see our lake freezing in cold winters and getting full of noises of happy children in summers. I can feel the smell of Polish summer. It was such a beautiful world. I will never stop mourning after this place and its community. Deep, deep inside, I will never stop dreaming that the war never came. A part of me remains there, running carefree in the quiet streets, learning Jewish traditions at home, school, and our beautiful synagogue. Growing peacefully, never inflicted with fear, never forced to any good bye, never forced to leave. A part of me will forever remain this young boy, whose life was so dramatically cut away.

Pupils in Szczekociny before the Second World War. The fourth from the right in the first row, sitting, Izyk Mendel Bornstein. The picture was found after the demise of Izyk Mendel Bornstein. Published by courtesy of Ms Jolanta Wojciechowska

Index

I

J

K

T

U

V

W

Y

Z

4817509R0

Made in the USA
Charleston, SC
21 March 2010